LIFE
HAPPENS

LIFE
HAPPENS

••

A Teenager's Guide to
Friends, Failure, Sexuality, Love,
Rejection, Addiction, Peer Pressure,
Families, Loss, Depression, Change,
and Other Challenges of Living

••

Kathy McCoy, Ph.D.,
and Charles Wibbelsman, M.D.

A PERIGEE BOOK

A Perigee Book
Published by The Berkley Publishing Group
200 Madison Avenue
New York, NY 10016

Book design by Rhea Braunstein
Cover design by Sheryl Kagan

First edition: March 1996

Published simultaneously in Canada.

The Putnam Berkley World Wide Web site address is
http://www.berkley.com

Library of Congress Cataloging-in-Publication Data
McCoy, Kathy.
    Life happens / Kathleen McCoy and Charles Wibblesman.
      p. cm.
    "A Perigee book."
    Summary: Offers advice on how to cope with such feelings as
sadness, anger, and anxiety related to various problems faced by
many teenagers.
    ISBN 0-399-51987-4
    1. Depression in adolescence. 2. Anxiety in adolescence.
3. Stress in adolescence. [1. Depression, Mental. 2. Stress
(Psychology). 3. Family problems.] I. Wibbelsman, Charles.
II. Title.
    RJ506.D4M324   1996   95-9647
    616.98'022—dc20   CIP
                                                         AC

PRINTED IN THE UNITED STATES OF AMERICA

10 9 8 7 6 5 4 3 2 1

CONTENTS

....

PART III
GETTING AND GIVING HELP

ACKNOWLEDGMENTS

Special thanks to . . .

- Our agent, Susan Ann Protter, who has seen us through so much in the past twenty years. We are grateful for her professional expertise and for her friendship, both of which have made a wonderful difference in both our lives.
- John Duff, the editor and publisher of this and several other of our books. John and his assistant Genny Wilkinson are a joy to know and to work with.
- Richard Holihan, M.D., for his inestimable contribution to this book in a way very special to both of us.
- Bob Stover for his love and caring, supportiveness and resourcefulness during the work on this book (and all the others)!
- Bill Farrell, M.A., a teacher and psychotherapist-

in-training, for his generous and invaluable suggestions and help in making this book as responsive as possible to teens' concerns. He is a valued colleague and treasured friend.

- Michael Scavio, Ph.D., and Patricia Le Sage, M.A., of the Clinical Ph.D. Program at California School of Professional Psychology (CSPP) in Los Angeles. As Kathy's boss and assistant respectively, they have demonstrated unfailing good humor, patience and warm support during her work on this book (especially as the final deadline loomed).

- Some other special people at CSPP who were unusually supportive of this project, including Chancellor Lisa Porche-Burke, Ph.D., Rosemary Abend, Ph.D., Tobeylynn Birch, M.L.S., Jan Wilson, M.L.S., Carlton Parks, Ph.D., Karen Finello, Ph.D., Elaine Burke, Psy.D., Jo Carr, Ph.D., Mal Bartlett, M.Div., Beverly Harman, Marci Arellano, Shelly Harrell, Ph.D., Richard Kopp, Ph.D., Sy Zelen, Ph.D., Ana Luisa Bustamante, Ph.D., Mona Delahooke, Ph.D., and Marilyn Mehr, Ph.D.

- Special friends, family and colleagues, including Tai Mareld, Mary Breiner, M.A., Tim Schellhardt, Carol Wilson, Jerry and Nancy Durham, M.A., Howard and Julie Anderson, Len and Judy Winokur, Tony Greenberg, M.D., Sister Ramona Bascom, Pat Hill, Caron Roudebush, Jack Hill, Andrea Cleghorn, Terrie Butorac, M.A., Greg Tse, M.A., Martha Carr, M.A., Reese Lawton, Ph.D., and Karin Hilsdale, Ph.D.

- Belated thanks to Liz Canfield, who introduced us and suggested our first collaboration many years ago, and to Bob MacLeod and Roxie Camron of *'TEEN* magazine for *everything!*
- Loving thanks to two very special aunts—Kathy's Aunt Elizabeth ("Molly") McCoy and Chuck's Aunt Angie Fisher. They have given us love, understanding, and support as "life happened"—in our teens and beyond.
- The teenagers quoted in these pages, who shared their pain and their healing, their insights and suggestions with us.

Part I

WHAT'S HAPPENING TO ME?

What Am I Feeling?
Why Do I Feel So Bad?

I feel totally alone and upset. My parents got divorced last year. They said they waited until I was fourteen and old enough to handle it (according to them!). Only I can't handle it. Mom and I had to move into this dumb apartment and I'm in a new school where I don't have any friends, after being fairly popular at my old school. Also, this probably sounds stupid, but it bothers me: my dog got hit and killed by a car last summer and I cry whenever I think of it, which makes me feel like a baby, but I can't help it. What scares me is that if I told anyone I know how bad I feel about what happened in my life this past year, they'd think I was crazy! *Am I crazy for feeling so bad?*

—Lost and Alone

Although the girl who wrote us this letter recently feels very much alone in her pain, she has a lot of company. We hear from many teens in pain: through letters written to us by readers of *The New Teenage Body Book,* from patients who share their emotional as well as physical pain and from young people we meet during visits to high schools, at seminars and in studio audiences of the many television shows and call-in radio shows we have done together. We also read between the lines of some sobering statistics about teens with a myriad of painful feelings.

Statistics show that one in three American teens is at risk for serious depression, according to a 1992 report by the Carnegie Council on Adolescent Development. And several recent studies have noted that gay and lesbian youth are at far greater risk for depression than their heterosexual peers. Children of divorced parents are also especially vulnerable to depression, according to Dr. Judith Wallerstein's many years of studies focused on families and divorce. She found that one-third of the children she studied were still experiencing moderate to severe levels of depression five years after a parental divorce.

Beyond statistics, there are individual stories of anguish and endurance.

There is Tara, sixteen, who can't shake her feelings of sadness and hopelessness "despite the fact that I supposedly have this great life. My parents are great. We have plenty of money. My grades are good and I have lots of friends. But there are times when I feel I have nothing to look forward to and I just feel like dying. If anyone knew I felt this way, I'd be called 'crazy' for sure!"

There is Shawn, a seventeen-year-old honor student, whose moments of anguish come when he is alone with his feelings of being pressured by his parents and teachers to get into an Ivy League college and his feelings of being different from peers, not just because some classmates label him a nerd for studying so hard, but also because he is quite certain that he is gay. "I haven't had sex with anyone yet," he says. "But I just know and it scares me. Not because I'm bad because of it, but because of the way my friends and family would react if they knew. So I walk around with this big secret and it hurts. I'm scared that everyone I love wouldn't love me back if they knew my secret."

There is Kyle, who has a serious learning disability and few friends. His academic limitations stand out painfully in his family: both parents are professionals and his older brother is making top grades in college. "I feel like I don't belong in my family," he says sadly. "I don't belong anywhere."

Feeling different, depressed, lost and alone can come as the result of a stressful life event or series of events or, seemingly, from nowhere.

If you're like most people, a large part of your pain is feeling that you're alone and afraid that if you let anyone know how bad you feel and why you feel that way (if you have a clue yourself), you'll be instantly branded as "crazy."

So you hide your feelings—pretending to be happy, pretending that life is going along as it always did—even though your heart is breaking and your spirit is being crushed by the darkness within.

Or you may deny your feelings or cover them up with angry or impulsive behavior. Without realizing what you're doing or why you're doing it, you may lash out at parents, family, friends or teachers, trying to discharge the hurt lodged deep inside. You may be trying to let people know, in an indirect way, that you're in emotional pain.

You might also try to deaden your feelings with alcohol, drugs, sex or eating disorders—again, not always realizing what you're doing and why.

The problem with these ways of dealing with painful feelings is that they will only add to your loneliness and depression.

If you hide your feelings, people who might help you don't know that you need them and you lose an opportunity to reach out for loving support.

If you cover your painful feelings with angry, impulsive behavior, you may get punishment instead of the understanding you need so much.

If you deal with painful feelings by running away—either from home or from feelings or situations that need to be resolved—you are simply prolonging your pain and complicating or even risking your life.

If you anesthetize your feelings with alcohol, drugs, sex or food, you put yourself at risk for more problems—some of them life-changing, even life-threatening.

What can you do when you're feeling so bad, so low, so hopeless that it's almost too much for you? How can you keep from making things worse for yourself instead of better?

Knowing what you're feeling is an important first step.

It isn't always easy to know exactly what you're feeling when you're feeling bad. All of us have ways of dealing with pain that keep us, at least for a time, from feeling overwhelmed by our problems. Alcohol, drugs, sex or food may be temporary ways of handling painful feelings for some people. Others try to ignore feelings of pain and discomfort by keeping too busy to reflect on how bad they're really feeling. Still others look to other people or to things to distract them: maybe shopping compulsively or partying nonstop, hanging out with friends all the time to avoid those uncomfortable moments alone or getting pregnant at an early age and expecting the baby to provide all the love and fulfillment they feel has been missing from their lives. Think about how you cope when you're feeling bad. If you've been reaching for temporary solutions that aren't helping, you're far from alone! It's very hard—especially when you're feeling bad—to take an honest look into what you're feeling. But it may be the only way to begin to feel better.

How can you start to get in touch with your feelings?

✓ *Spend some time alone, exploring your feelings.* Make time to be alone and think. Maybe this will be in your room, with your favorite CD playing. Or you might take a walk to a quiet place where you feel peaceful and safe. (The exercise may help you feel better and think clearly as an added bonus.) Or just take a deep breath right now, right where you are. Close your eyes and let your body relax from your toes to the top of your head. As you become aware of your body's physical sensations of relaxation, become aware of your feelings right now, too. Accept these feelings and give each a name. Is what you're feeling sadness? Anger? A feeling of hopelessness, that life will never get any better? Are you feeling lonely? Rejected? Left out? Anxious? Stressed out? Scared because you fear no one will like or accept you if they *really know* who you are? While it can be painful to get in touch with these feelings, knowing what you're feeling is a vital clue and a first step to changing your life for the better. (And, as hopeless as life may feel right now, it *can* get better!)

✓ *Tap your creativity for special insights.* Especially if you find your feelings difficult to pinpoint, let your creativity lead the way. Start a journal, writing what's going on (or not going on) in your life, your feelings and your dreams. Even if you don't consider yourself a writer (and have English grades to prove it!), writing about your feelings—for your eyes only—can give you new insights and, at times, a sense of relief. For example, you might want to vent your anger at a boyfriend or girlfriend who left you or at a parent who just can't seem to understand you. Expressing your anger in writing, just for yourself, can be a way of beginning to deal with these feelings and to find new, more positive ways to handle that troubling relationship. If you enjoy writing poetry, that can be an excellent way to discover and express what you're feeling. If you freeze at the thought of putting pen to paper, but are talented in art or music, drawing a picture inspired by your feelings or composing (or choosing to listen to) a song that best expresses what you're feeling right now can give you some valuable clues to your feelings.

✓ *Talk with someone—not for answers but to explore what you're feeling.* This person might be a friend, a parent, a family member, your doctor, a favorite teacher, a youth group leader from your church—but someone you trust and who is a good listener. You might start off with "I'm feeling really bad, but I'm not sure why . . ."

Someone who knows you well may help you to come up with words to express your feelings. If you're too embarrassed right now to talk with a person (and you're not feeling desperate, but definitely blue), talk to a beloved pet. (People of all ages do and many find this quite comforting.) But if you're feeling hopeless and maybe even beginning to think about suicide, tell an adult who can help or lead you to a source of help. Or call a youth hot line or local suicide prevention center hot line for immediate help and referral to a professional counselor who will help you to sort out your feelings and find new hope.

✓ *Don't dismiss your feelings as "crazy."* Accept your feelings as they are without labeling them "crazy" or "bad." Sometimes feelings *seem* not quite logical—like feeling lonely in a crowd or feeling down during a time of great success in your life—but there is always a reason for your feelings that simply can't be judged. It's perfectly natural to feel lonely in a crowd if everyone else is in a couple and you have no one special or if, for some other reason, you feel you don't fit in. And finding yourself in tears and feeling down just after something wonderful happens may be a sign that you're experiencing the loss of a long-time goal. Many teens, for example, may feel a letdown at the end of senior year, when all the fun and much-anticipated milestones have come and gone or when they have been accepted to the college of their choice (after a really intense application process) and are thinking "Now what?" as they prepare to start over again in a new school setting.

So if you're feeling bad in the middle of a happy time, you're not crazy. And if you're feeling bad in the middle of a difficult period of your life, you're not crazy. Feeling pain as well as joy is simply part of being human. Accepting the whole range of your feelings as normal can help you to feel less alone and better able to help yourself—or ask for help from others.

✓ *Treat yourself like a dear friend.* What would you say or do if a close friend came to you and told you that he or she was feeling troubled? Chances are, you wouldn't say, "You're crazy! You're really stupid to feel that way!" or "Well, what do you expect? You always (say the wrong thing, pick the wrong person to love, do things to upset your math teacher, etc., etc.)." Even if your friend did have a penchant for loving people who didn't love him or her back or had a chronic case of foot-in-mouth syndrome, you would find a more caring way to explore this: "You have so much love to give . . . I would love to see you meet someone who would really appreciate you. Why do you think you have been attracted to people recently who *couldn't* love you the way you needed and wanted to be loved? What did you like about that person? What would you have liked to be different about that relationship? What would you like to be different next time? How do you think you can help make things different?"

It's important to treat yourself as gently and as non-judgmentally as you would a treasured friend. Only then will you feel safe and secure enough to let yourself know, accept and experience your feelings fully and begin to heal your pain.

....

2

What Does It Mean
to Be Depressed?

Depression can happen in a variety of ways and for many different reasons. At times, what some people call "depression" is not depression at all.

For example, when Sara, sixteen, lost her mother to cancer last year, she felt a confusing mixture of anger, guilt and grief. As she cried her way through the weeks following her mother's death, her friends worried about her depression. But what Sara was experiencing was the grief process—which can include anger at the person for dying and leaving you, guilt about what you could or should have done for or said to that person before he or she died and an incredible sense of sadness and loss. This is a somewhat predictable response to a major loss.

In other instances—the loss of a love relationship, the loss of a goal through failure to make that goal (not making a team at school or not getting into the college of your choice)—there can be a sense of loss, some grieving and a depressed mood for a time. But that is not the same as a major depression that can overwhelm you for reasons you don't always understand.

Depression is often used as a sort of catchall phrase to describe a variety of symptoms. It is often the result of a complex mix of social, psychological and/or physical factors that can trigger sadness, hopelessness and feelings of inferiority, powerlessness and helplessness. While some people experience depression after a major loss or setback—when it becomes grief that just won't quit—others experience these feelings for reasons that are not clear-cut. For some, depression can be a lifelong illness that comes and goes in a recurring cycle.

TYPES OF DEPRESSION

Depressed Mood

Maybe you're feeling unhappy because of a specific event: not making a team or not winning an academic honor or not getting a job you had wanted. Or you may be feeling down because of a romantic breakup, a parental divorce, the death of a pet or a family move that has taken you away from your friends and forced you to start over.

You may experience a depressed mood suddenly in response to a loss situation. It may be relatively brief—a few days or a few weeks—or it may occur over an extended period of time. But it is usually linked directly to a specific situation and is quite identifiable as sadness or unhappiness.

Clinical Depression

This term is used to describe depression that is more persistent and severe, that has a variety of symptoms and may not be as easily linked to a specific cause as a depressed mood might be.

There are several major types of clinical depression as described by the American Psychiatric Association in the *DSM-IV,* a diagnostic guide published in 1994 for physicians, psychologists and other mental health professionals. The types of clinical depression include the following:

Major Depressive Disorder, Single Episode or Recurrent

To be diagnosed with a major depressive disorder, you must have suffered from five or more of the following specific symptoms for more than two weeks in a way that interferes with your daily life. These symptoms include:

1. Depressed or irritable mood most of the day, nearly every day
2. Loss of interest or pleasure in activities you have previously enjoyed
3. Significant weight loss (without dieting) or weight gain (a change of more than 5 percent of body weight in one month), diminished or increased appetite; also, if you do not make expected weight gains during puberty as your body grows and matures, this, too, can be an important sign of trouble.

4. Insomnia (difficulty sleeping) or hypersomnia (sleeping too much) nearly every day
5. Feelings of restlessness or being slowed down
6. Feelings of fatigue and loss of energy nearly every day
7. Feelings of worthlessness or excessive or inappropriate guilt on a daily basis
8. Diminished ability to think or concentrate, or persistent indecisiveness nearly every day
9. Recurrent thoughts of death (not just fear of dying), thoughts of suicide with or without a specific plan, and/or suicide attempts

Some people have a single episode of major depression. Others experience a number of depressive episodes (separated by at least two months in which the person does not have symptoms of a major depressive episode).

Dysthymic Disorder

Depressed teens with dysthymic disorder experience depressive symptoms for at least one year (and have not been without symptoms for longer than two months at a time), but this may or may not have as severe an impact on daily life as major depressive disorder.

The symptoms, which must be present for most of the day, nearly every day, for a year or more include:

1. Poor appetite or overeating
2. Sleep problems—sleeping too much or insomnia
3. Low energy level and fatigue
4. Low self-esteem

5. Poor concentration or difficulty making decisions
6. Feelings of hopelessness

Teens with dysthymic disorder are usually cranky and irritable most days, as well as being depressed. They have trouble relating to peers and to adults and tend to be chronically pessimistic.

Bipolar Disorder

Classified, like depression, as a mood disorder, bipolar disorder in teens causes the young person to have mood swings that vary well beyond the usual changeable moods of adolescence. The young person with bipolar disorder has moods that alternate between manic, or highly energetic—during which he or she is agitated, sleeps little, talks incessantly, has boundless energy and inflated self-esteem—and major depression.

A chronic form of bipolar disorder is called *cyclothymia*. Here, the teen has had bipolar episodes for at least a year without more than a two-month respite from symptoms.

WHY ARE WE TELLING YOU THIS?

These descriptions of major depression and related mood disorders are not meant to scare you into the conviction that you really *are* crazy, abnormal or easily categorized.

What we hope you'll understand as the result of reading this chapter is that depression happens for a lot of reasons—none of them because you are crazy or bad or ungrateful or ornery. Some of the reasons—as we will see in the next chapter—are easily identified as losses in your life. Others—which can include a genetic predisposition for depression—are more difficult to pinpoint.

We also hope this will show you that you are not alone. If mental health professionals see these symptoms enough to put them into categories with diagnostic names, it means that thousands of teens have shared many quite similar painful feelings and symptoms and that there are people who can understand and help— even though life may feel pretty hopeless to you right now.

....

3

What's Happening in My Life to Make Me Feel So Bad?

Amy twists a crumpled tissue around in her hand as she speaks slowly, hesitantly, barely holding back tears.

"I don't know why I'm feeling so bad right now," she says softly. "All the bad stuff is behind me. My parents got divorced a year ago and life isn't great, but it's OK. The apartment my mom and I moved to is OK. I'm not fighting as much with my mom. I'm not as mad at my dad as I was a year ago. Some people at my new school have been pretty friendly. So it's better, but I feel worse. I cry at the slightest thing. I can hardly get out of bed in the morning. I feel down about things that didn't used to bother me. Am I going crazy or is something else seriously wrong with me?"

Amy is not going crazy, but she *is* reacting to a series of stressful and painful events in her life. In the past year, her parents have divorced. She and her mother moved from a suburban house to a city apartment, and Amy changed schools. She rarely sees her father, with whom she was close and who has just remarried. Even though (or actually *because*) the shock has worn off, Amy is in a lot of pain from the series of losses and changes she has experienced in a relatively short time.

The same may be true for you.

Even if things have happened that you've nearly forgotten, even if you don't think of a painful event or series of events as catastrophic, even if you think of a painful loss only once or twice a day instead of a hundred times a day, it can all add up to depression, grief and an ongoing feeling of loss. It doesn't take a life-changing event like the death of someone you love or a parental divorce. Little stresses in your life can add up and cause increased vulnerability to depression.

HOW VULNERABLE ARE YOU TO DEPRESSION?

If you answer yes with a check to even one of the following, you may be quite familiar with sad or angry feelings. If you answer yes to several—and these events have occurred within the past year or so—you're especially likely to experience depression.

❏ Has anyone in your immediate or close extended family died during the past year?

❏ Has the family pet died or been lost?

❏ Have you lost a friend through death in the past year?

❏ Has a close friend moved away in the past year?

❏ Have you been rejected, abandoned, betrayed by or estranged from a close friend in the past year?

❏ Have you had a recent (or fairly recent) breakup with a boyfriend or girlfriend?

❏ Have your parents separated or divorced in the past year or two?

❏ If your parents have divorced, do you see one or the other much less frequently than before?

❏ Have your parents been having marital problems (or fighting a lot more than usual) in the past year?

❏ Has one (or both) of your parents become unemployed, or even if they're employed, are financial problems a fact of life for your family recently?

❏ Has your family moved within the past twelve months?

❏ Have you changed schools in the past year—either due to a move or due to progressing on to junior high, high school or college?

❏ Has a brother or sister left home for college, marriage or independent living?

❏ Has a parent, brother or sister experienced serious depression in the past year or two?

❏ Has any extended family member—grandparent, aunt, uncle, cousin—suffered from depressive illness?

❏ Do you have an alcoholic or drug-abusing parent or parents?

❏ Has anyone in your immediate family had a serious illness or injury in the past year?

❏ Have you had an illness or injury in the past year that limited your normal activities?

❏ Do you have a chronic illness such as diabetes or

epilepsy that might affect your participation in activities with your friends or that may be a source of conflict between you and your parents?

❑ Has your body changed fairly dramatically in the past year—e.g., have you grown a lot taller, had your voice change, started menstruating or had noticeable breast development—and been teased about all this?

❑ Are you behind or ahead of your friends in terms of physical development—and do you get teased or picked on because of this?

❑ Has your family had a major change of life-style recently, due to financial hardships, parental job loss or a parent reentering the job market?

❑ Do you tend to be very self-critical and generally have a low opinion of yourself?

❑ Do your parents expect a lot of you and get obviously upset and disappointed when you fall short of their expectations?

❑ Is someone in your family extremely critical of you? Do other family members tend to agree or disagree with this person about you?

❑ Are you finding it really hard to communicate with your parents lately—and, deep inside, do you miss the closeness you used to have?

❑ Do you have a learning disability?

❑ Do you have difficulty making or keeping friends?

❑ Do you think (or know) that you are gay or lesbian—or, if you're not into labels, do you find that you are attracted to someone of the same sex—and have you not felt able to share this part of yourself with some significant people in your life?

❏ Do you sometimes have the feeling that because your parents have few rules, they don't really care about you?

❏ Do you feel smothered and overwhelmed by parents who are very strict and don't allow you to express your opinions or show anger—ever?

❏ Is someone close to you abusing you—either emotionally or physically? (This could be a parent, sibling, boyfriend, girlfriend or close relative.)

❏ Have you been sexually abused?

❏ Do people at school gang up on you and ridicule, tease or generally single you out for a hard time?

❏ Are you a perfectionist—getting really upset when you do something or make a grade that is less than the best? Do you feel like a total failure at such times?

❏ Are you having difficulty with a particular teacher this year?

❏ Has a parent remarried, bringing a stepparent into the family, within the last two years?

❏ Has your immediate family had an addition—the birth of a brother or sister, grandparents or other relatives moving in—that has increased your level of household responsibilities or decreased your privacy?

❏ Has a brother or sister made a significant achievement in the past year or so that has shifted parental attention away from your accomplishments and/or caused your parents to compare you unfavorably to your sibling?

❏ Have *you* achieved a significant goal recently, such as graduating, winning an award, making a team, perfecting a skill, getting into the college of your choice or winning some other unusual recognition? (Sometimes success can be bittersweet as you lose a long-held goal by achieving it!)

You can be vulnerable to depression because of a series of changes, losses or stresses in your life despite the fact that, at the moment, life may be fairly OK. Or a crisis may push you over the edge into a deep, dark emotional abyss. Some of the depression-triggering crises we hear most often from teens include the following:

LOSS OF A LOVE

This sense of loss may happen not only in the wake of a romantic breakup, but also when a boyfriend or girlfriend moves away or goes off to college and, as letters get fewer and silences on the phone get longer, you worry that the love that you both were sure would last forever won't survive until Christmas vacation.

This sense of loss of love can stretch to include best friends who move away, or reject you for new best friends, or become so involved with a romantic relationship that they forget all about close nonromantic friends. And you wonder if all those times of sharing secrets or

playing sports together or just hanging out meant anything—whether *you* meant anything at all to your former
friend.

EXPERIENCING A FAILURE (or Feeling Like a Failure)

If you have failed to fulfill one of your own dreams or
goals or one or more of your parents' goals for you, you
may be feeling pretty low right now. Failure hurts most
when you don't confine your feelings of having failed to
a specific behavior, talent or event and instead believe
that you are an abject failure as a person. Life can look
hopeless, and you may be feeling helpless to change anything.

It can also be a helpless feeling when, for reasons you
can't really pin down, no one at school wants to be your
friend. In fact, people may shun you, make fun of you
and generally make your life miserable when all you're
doing is trying to be a good person and get through
high school. You may feel like a failure when no one will
eat lunch with you, when others tease you or simply
when everyone else at school seems to have it together—
physically, socially and emotionally—except you. If
you're feeling that the same clothes that look great on
everyone else make you look even more geeky, if every
day is a bad hair day and you're convinced that you're
the only person you know who manages to totally em-
barrass himself or herself at least once or twice a day, it's
all too easy to feel like a failure (even though you're
not!).

FAMILY CHANGES AND PROBLEMS

Family changes and problems can have a huge impact on your life. A move, of course, can mean leaving friends behind and changing schools—perhaps totally against your will—and you feel powerless and angry as well as sad at all the losses the move has meant for you. The illness or disability of a sibling can be stressful and sad for you: while you may feel fear, love and sadness for your sibling, you may also feel left out and neglected when so much of the family energy focuses on your brother or sister. Of course, if your parents are experiencing problems, these can't help but touch your life in a major way: an alcoholic or drug-abusing parent or parents who fight all the time or a parental divorce can affect your feelings and your life for years to come. Even an event that your parents consider positive—like a remarriage or the birth of a new baby, especially within a newly blended family—may be a mixed blessing for you as you experience, perhaps, a loss of parental attention and an increase in family responsibility.

SEXUALITY-RELATED FEELINGS AND PROBLEMS

Whether or not you actually have sex as a teen, sexuality—which can include feelings as well as actions—is newly important and, at times, problematic in adolescence. You may be feeling pressured by a boyfriend or a girlfriend to have sex before you feel ready—and you're scared both of losing the relationship and losing your self-respect by going against some of your own values.

You may be experiencing a pregnancy scare or may actually be pregnant—and feel desperate and very much alone. Or you may suspect or know for sure that you are gay or lesbian and feel a lot of uneasiness, depression and anger as you debate whether to share who you are with your family and friends—or as you experience a variety of reactions, not all of them positive, from those you love most.

SOMEONE YOU LOVE HAS DIED

When you lose someone you love—a parent, another relative, a dear friend or a family pet (a loss *not* to be minimized!)—you may wonder if you'll ever feel happy again. Grief can be a difficult emotional and physical process, as you grapple with feelings from denial to anger to desperate longing and sadness to acceptance. The process isn't an even one: you may feel better one day and just horrible the next (and wonder, in the process, if you're losing your mind). And if you get stuck somewhere in the process and grief turns into ongoing depression, you may be wondering if life will ever feel normal again.

YOU FEEL AWFUL AND YOU DON'T KNOW WHY

Sometimes, despite trying to pinpoint your feelings and the causes for these feelings and talking to those closest to you, you can't figure out why you're feeling so bad—and that can *really* make you wonder about yourself! The fact is, sometimes depression can have a physical or a chemical cause. As we will discuss later on, if you're feeling bad and you don't know why, it's vital to talk with your physician—to see if you might have a condition like mononucleosis that is contributing to your feelings of depression and fatigue—and to a mental health professional—to see if your depression may be due to chemical (perhaps genetically linked) processes that can be treated with medication and psychotherapy.

SOMEONE YOU LOVE IS IN A CRISIS

If you have a friend or family member who is going through an emotional, depressive crisis and you're not sure how to help, you may feel scared, sad, even desperate as you worry that this person you love will not make it through this crisis without harming himself or herself, perhaps irrevocably. You wonder whether to tell anyone else, whom to tell and how to get the help your loved one so desperately needs—and, all through this, you feel the full weight and urgency of his or her pain.

Whether the one in crisis is you or someone you love, the following chapters will give you some ideas for figuring out what is happening, what you're feeling and how to deal with the feelings in a life-enhancing way.

Part II

COMMON CRISES—AND HOW TO HELP YOURSELF

4

I've Loved and Lost (and Other Hazards of Love Relationships)

I was going with Ashley, but then she left me for someone else and I feel like an idiot because all my friends told me that this would happen and I wouldn't believe them because I cared so much for her. Right now, I feel like I'll never be happy again and I'm mad at her and jealous of Sean, the guy she's seeing. How can I get over this? How can I feel so bad about losing someone who (my friends say) was no good for me in the first place?
—Ted R.

A breakup is totally horrible, especially if you're gay because everyone is glad! They think it means "You're over that phase! Now you're going to be 'normal' " and that makes it hurt ten times as much. How can I start feeling better?
—Sad in San Jose

I never thought it would be true, but it is: it's really hard to be the one to break up with someone you care about.

My boyfriend is a freshman at a college two thousand miles away and we haven't seen each other since he left, though he will be coming home for Christmas soon and I have to tell him that I've met and become involved with someone else. I've tried to hint about it in letters but he has been sounding so lonely and so eager to see me again for the holidays that I didn't have the heart to come out with it. Every time I think about breaking up with him, I cry, but I know it's the best thing—at least for me. Is it normal to feel so bad about being the one to break up?

—Deb K.

I can't stop crying because my boyfriend just dumped me for my best friend. I feel like I've lost everyone *who's really important in my life. Why would people who* said *they loved and liked me hurt me so much—and on purpose?? What can I do in revenge so I can feel better?*

—Brittany Y.

The situations in these letters vary widely, but the basic experience and the feelings are the same: a feeling of profound loss when you lose an important love.

You may feel shock, sadness, anger, a hole in your life and your heart. You may feel wistful, lonely, resentful and unloved. You may feel especially bad if your pain is not shared or at least validated by those close to you: if, like "Sad in San Jose," your family is relieved that your relationship is over, or if your parents seem terribly casual about your loss—as in "It was just puppy love!" or "There will be others. Next week you won't even remember his (her) name because you'll be in love with someone else." But that's *not* the way it is. When you hear a song that was special to the two of you, walk by a place you used to go together, have vivid memories from your loving past or your unhappy ending as a couple that come back again and again or, worst of all, see your former love with someone new, you may feel so bad you can't imagine ever feeling better. Like Brittany, you may plot revenge—but lack the energy (or the nerve) to carry it out. You may wonder if you've just been used, if anyone will ever *really* love you, if there is one person on this earth that you can trust. You may find yourself wondering if you'll ever love another person as much again.

If you're on the *other* side of a breakup, this can be a painful time, too. As Deb says in her letter, it's hard to be the one to break up and to hurt someone who has meant a lot to you but who is simply not the right person for you right now—or maybe ever. You, too, may feel a variety of feelings. You may experience guilt as you think about telling him or her that it's over, or as you watch your soon-to-be-ex-love's painful reaction to the news. You may feel anger if he or she refuses to believe or accept your feelings, or if he or she angrily berates you and, perhaps out of hurt and self-defense, claims that the relationship wasn't worth having anyway. You may feel fear because your ex-love is even physically threatening or harassing you. And you may wonder, with new urgency, what you can do to end this relationship once and for all.

Or you may be facing a romantic breakup of a relationship that *can't* really end because you're in all the same classes and some teachers favor alphabetical seating which puts your ex-love right next to you (which is how

you got to know each other in the first place!); or because you're co-editors of the school newspaper and
you've got about ten more issues to go before you can
even contemplate a parting of the ways; or because your
ex-love is part of your extended family or your everyday
life, such as your married sister's husband's younger
brother or, quite literally, the girl next door; or maybe
you were friends before you fell in love and you'd like
to be friends again . . . if only you could get past all the
hurt . . .

These are just some of the feelings and the challenges
that a romantic breakup can bring.

What can you do if you find yourself facing some of
these?

IF YOUR LOVE HAS LEFT YOU

✓ *Allow yourself a period of grief.* Grief is a natural reaction to loss, and tears can be healing. Let this natural
process happen. Cry if you feel like it—even if you're a
guy. It's OK and normal to cry when you're hurting—
either alone or with trusted friends or a therapist. Let
yourself feel the pain, from denial to anger to passing
depression—you will heal faster and, perhaps, be
stronger. But be selective in where and with whom you
let your grief reactions happen. Choose a compassionate
friend or relative who can understand your pain. You
don't need someone telling you what a total jerk your
ex-love was and how everyone knew he (or she) was just
using you, or, even worse (this is a favorite of many
adults), going on about how it wasn't really love, just a

teen crush or "puppy love" (whatever *that* may be!). You probably know the people who will listen without judgment and who care more about you than about being relentlessly right. Seek these people out when you need a friendly shoulder, and also give yourself the time to grieve in private.

✓ *Use your creative skills to work through your grief.* If you keep a journal, it can help to write about your feelings, especially the ones you're too shy or ashamed to share with others right now. If you haven't kept a journal, now might be a good time to start one. Play music that parallels your mood or helps you get past tears to hope again (upbeat music can be a first step in lightening your mood). Draw how it feels to lose a love. Write a letter to the person who left you and then tear it up. Getting those feelings out and then letting them go is to *your* benefit.

✓ *Think about the negative aspects of the relationship.* It can be tempting, as you grieve your loss, to think of all the wonderful aspects of the relationship and what you'll miss about the other person. To get new perspective, think for a moment about what you *won't* miss: the little faults and habits you struggled to overlook, the things you fought about, the compromises you made for the relationship that you won't choose to make again. We learn from all of our relationships, and part of that learning is finding out what we *don't* want, what we can live with and what we can't. If you think about it, this relationship has probably been a valuable learning experience in that regard.

✓ *See the positive aspects of the relationship in a new way.*
It's entirely normal, as part of the grieving process, to
feel sad when you think of all the good times you and
your ex-love shared and all the things you're going to
miss about him or her. But as you begin to feel a little
stronger, take a new look at these positive times as enduring gifts in your life. Maybe your love helped you to
develop an interest or a skill or to discover a new pleasure that you wouldn't have otherwise. For example, he
or she might have turned you on to the joys of hiking
or cycling, or may have encouraged your musical talents.
Maybe your love helped you get more motivated in your
classes or more involved in community activities or excited about a career possibility you hadn't dared to consider before. Or maybe the legacy of the relationship is
a collage of happy, very special memories: sitting on the
beach sharing secrets and life plans; taking turns reading
to each other from *The Wind in the Willows* and discovering a whole new twist to this childhood classic; crack-
ing silly jokes that only the two of you can hear on a
crowded dance floor; getting caught in a sudden rain-
storm, laughing as you both get drenched, taking shelter
under a store's awning and kissing with exquisite tenderness (between bouts of laughter); the delicious feeling of being understood and accepted—whether it was
your love getting excited over an idea you had that
everyone else said was silly, or having the experience of
your loved one seeing you at less than your best and
loving you anyway.

The fact is, while you may lose a love, you do not
have to lose the gifts that that person, that relationship,
gave you. If you choose, you can quietly thank him or

her for these revelations, happy memories and good times. No two relationships are the same. You may never again have quite the same set of experiences with another—but embracing this joy will keep you open to experiencing new pleasures alone *and* with others.

✓ *Forgive the other person—and yourself.* It isn't simply a matter of "Forgive and forget!" because you never do forget a first or early love. But forgiving is vital. Anger and rage can happen when a love walks out of your life, but you need to forgive in order to be free to go on with your life. Forgiving does not mean saying that the other person was right or that he or she didn't hurt you. It means letting go of your outrage over the other person's behavior—not, of course, on day one, but after you've had time to work through your grief. You might acknowledge that people make the choices they do for reasons that others may never understand, and decide to forgive your ex-love the choices that hurt you.

Forgiving yourself is also an important aspect of this process. Part of the burden of grief you may be carrying could be a big load of "If only's": "If only I had done this . . . hadn't done that . . . he (she) wouldn't have left me . . . It's all my fault . . . I'm not a good, attractive, lovable person." It *is* useful to look at possible contributions you may have made to the breakup. Such self-reflection is part of your learning process—learning what you might do better or differently next time—instead of something to beat yourself over the head about for the next fifty years. Hanging on to anger or remorse keeps you tied to your pain and to the past. Forgiving helps you let go, grow in new ways and, someday, take the risk of loving again.

IF YOU'RE THE ONE WHO WANTS TO BREAK UP

✓ *If you know the relationship isn't going to work, break up sooner rather than later.* Some people, afraid of hurting another's feelings, procrastinate endlessly when it comes to breaking up, hoping that the other person will lose interest first. And so the relationship goes on . . . and the hurt is greater when the breakup does come. The only exception we can imagine would be if the other person is going through an unusually stressful time: a parent is on the verge of death or has just died, or the person is on the edge of a suicidal depression. This doesn't mean you should be held hostage to a person just because his or her life is painful right now. But you might choose to be a good friend, emphasizing the friendship part, until the crisis has passed, and then break up as gently as possible.

✓ *Be honest yet gentle.* It's best to let the person know that the relationship isn't working for *you* and not to hold out false hopes that this could change in the future. That said, there are many ways to express this sentiment. Saying something like "You're a very good person, but at this point in my life, I want to go out with others and I feel that this relationship isn't for me" may hurt . . . but hurt less than saying "I want to break up with you because you're boring, ugly, not at all my type and I've found someone better!" Being gently honest and direct about your feelings is also better than simply making excuses about why you're busy rather than available, or just disappearing from that person's life with no warnings or explanations.

✓ *Think before you say "Let's just be friends."* Do you want to be friends with this person? If you don't—and you're offering friendship to relieve your own guilt—you may end up hurting the person more. If you do want a friendship and are unhappily surprised by the other's angry reaction to or rejection of that possibility, keep in mind that it takes time to get over the pain of rejection and loss and to think about making a major shift in the relationship. The best candidates for such a change are those who were good friends before they ever had a romantic relationship. Then, it isn't a matter of being "just" friends (a distinction that minimizes the real treasure of friendship), but of continuing and rediscovering, in time, the joys of friendship.

✓ *Be kind but be firm about boundaries.* You need to let your ex-love know that you care about his or her feelings, but that it isn't OK to call you constantly (or in the middle of the night), follow you around or create scenes at school or when you're with another person. Setting an example, you may also take care not to get directly involved with your ex-love's life. Just because you could tell him or her everything doesn't mean that it's OK for you to call and bend his or her ear about your difficulties with your new love, or that it's wise to pass judgment on anyone else your ex-love may go out with. You need to give each other the space and privacy to go on, and realize that, even if you are planning to continue your friendship, it takes time for the relationship to change—and people don't change at the same rate. You need to establish some limits in your friendship. Maybe these mean enjoying each other as friends, but taking care not to meddle in each other's love lives or to criticize new loves or to expect to share *all* the details of your friend's life.

✓ *Forgive yourself—and the other person.* It can feel awful to hurt another person—especially someone who has meant a lot to you—but this doesn't make you a terrible person. It can be much more hurtful to stay with someone, pretending you care about him or her because you're afraid of hurting that person or because you don't want to be alone. You need to forgive yourself for hurting another and for your part in the relationship not working out. You also need to forgive the other person—both for not being right for you (it's amazing how angry you can feel when you discover this, and you may go through a period of wishing the other person would change, or actively trying to change that person in ways he or she simply can't be changed) and for any anger and blame shown during your breakup. People in pain say things that, quite often, they don't really mean (or they mean it at the time, but not a few hours later). Give the person the benefit of the doubt and let it go. Letting this hurt go can free you to go on with your life—perhaps a little wiser and more compassionate than you were before.

IF YOU'VE BROKEN UP—BUT YOUR RELATIONSHIP MUST GO ON

✓ *Decide on the limits and possibilities of your relationship—together or apart.* Not all former love relationships that demand further ties for permanent or relatively temporary reasons are destined to become close friendships.

It may be that the best possible outcome would be to forgive one another and then to be civil and polite to each other when you do find yourselves together.

In other instances, a mandatory tie can be a blessing, forcing you to come to terms with your losses and forge a new relationship. For example, Katie Martin and Ben Martindale met because of alphabetical seating in their history class. When their dating relationship broke up, they were chagrined to find themselves sitting, side by side, in not one, but two new classes. "But it meant we had to make peace and stop fighting in order to stand being together," says Katie. "It really helped us to get over our hurt feelings and start to be friends again." And one young couple we know who were forced to work together on a long research project after their tempestuous breakup say that what initially felt like a life sentence became a loving friendship built to last a lifetime. In between all the initial fighting and tears and the completion of their project came new understanding and appreciation for each other as people and as friends.

✓ *Give the relationship time to change.* Going through a breakup in close proximity to each other does not mean bypassing all the elements of grief, pain and anger that are most often part of a breakup. There may be tears, some arguments, hurt feelings and growing pains as your relationship shifts to one of distant cordiality or to an ongoing, platonic friendship. It's important to be gentle with each other in transition—especially when you have to be in such close proximity—and to give each other time and room to adapt to the change.

✓ *Enjoy what is instead of longing for what was.* You tried hard to make your love relationship work and it simply was not to be. Few realities of life are more painful. Perhaps right now the possibility of enjoying this person in another role seems remote. But as friendship is a great blessing in love, love can add incredible richness and tenderness to a friendship. Think about the possibilities. If the best you can hope for is a distant yet respectful and cordial relationship, that still can be a positive factor in your life—especially if you have family ties. If a loving friendship is possible, it can be a great blessing, occupying a very special place in your heart and your life.

WHEN YOU NEED EXTRA HELP...

When time, tears and reflection haven't healed your pain, you may need extra help to recover from this loss and get on with your life.

How do you know you may need extra help? You need help when:

COMMON CRISES / 41

- Your feelings of sadness, depression and loss are just as strong after several weeks or even months as they were the first day of your breakup.
- You have become obsessed with your lost love: you call him all the time, follow her everywhere, can't get that person out of your mind . . . and this is something you can't seem to control.
- There are times when you fantasize about doing something terrible to the other person—just to get even—and lately you've slipped from fantasizing to planning.
- You left an abusive relationship, but are thinking of going back to him or her because you're scared that he or she will harm you if you don't.
- Your pain and loss has turned into depression and a sense of hopelessness. There are times when you think life isn't worth living without your love and you're feeling that suicide might be the only way to stop your pain.

Keep in mind that you're not crazy if you're experiencing any or all of these feelings. It just means that you need a little extra support right now. How and where can you get this?

✓ *Share your feelings and continuing pain with those you love and trust, including adults.* If you're like many teens, you've let your friends know how devastated you feel but you might not have told a parent or a teacher or another adult friend. If you find the pain hanging on, now is the time to seek support from trusted adults as well as friends. They may be able to help you find coping strategies that work especially well for you, or to find some kind of professional help if they feel you need it. Adults who love you are not likely to make fun of your feelings or minimize your pain if you let them know how deeply this breakup is hurting you and how much you need their help. Losing a first or very special love is an almost universal experience: we've all been there and can understand—to an extent—what you're going through. Sometimes, it just helps to know that others understand how you're feeling, and care.

✓ *Seek professional help if your depression persists or if you're having destructive thoughts.* This would include being so obsessed with your lost love that the rest of your life is falling apart, or getting so into plotting revenge that some of your fantasies are beginning to seem like scary plans. Professional help is also in order if you're feeling hopeless or suicidal.

✓ *Resist the temptation to return to an abusive partner out of fear or guilt.* No one deserves to be abused. Whether your previous love was so verbally abusive that you ended up feeling horrible about yourself, or was actually physically abusive—pushing or shoving you, beating you or forcing you to have sex when you didn't want to—the fact remains that you were abused and there is no good reason for you or anyone else to be the target for such treatment—ever. Going back out of fear means returning to the nightmare—and never being without fear that the abuse will happen again. Going back out of guilt—maybe your former love says he or she is *really* sorry this time and has been so sweet—means going back into a cycle where you can only lose. Abusers have a cycle of behavior: the buildup of tension in the relationship, the abuse and then a "honeymoon" period of heartfelt apologies, promises that it will never happen again and all manner of courtship behavior—flowers, gifts, cards, letters, winsome smiles and wonderful kisses—to win back your love. Then the whole cycle will start over again. An abuser will not change without professional help—and even then, the prognosis isn't always hopeful. And unfortunately, many of the people who most need help are very resistant to getting it. If you have been abusive in your relationship, it's vital to accept the fact that it *will* happen again—despite all your promises and good intentions—unless you decide to get therapy and work very hard to understand why this behavior is happening and how to stop the cycle. If you have been a victim, therapy can help, too. It can help you understand why you may be attracted to abusive people, what you can do to stop being a victim and how to make choices that are more beneficial to you (because, like everyone else, you *deserve* to be treated with love and with respect).

✓ *Take vacations from your pain.* While it can be life-enhancing—even life-saving—to get professional help to deal with your ongoing pain, it can also be useful, at times, to give yourself a break and a little vacation from your pain. This means choosing not to dwell on your loss for ten minutes, an hour or even a few hours. It can mean choosing to do something you would normally enjoy—and giving yourself permission to feel joy in doing it again. It can mean acting, for a short time, as if you hadn't suffered this loss. You might decide to go see a comedy movie or to spend some time laughing with family and friends, or simply let your sense of humor take over and give you some much-needed perspective. Learning to laugh between your moments of pain can give you new strength to deal with the pain when it returns, and new hope that you will get through this difficult time—and, someday, love again.

5

I Feel Like a Failure

It can be as specific as not making the basketball team or not having a date to the prom, not winning a class election or bombing out socially or academically at a new school. It can be as general as feeling that *nothing* you do turns out right, that you're always disappointing yourself or your parents, that there is nothing special about being you.

Whatever the cause, feelings of failure can be very painful. What can you do when you're feeling like a failure?

✓ *Ask yourself why you're feeling like a failure and give yourself an on-the-spot quiz, asking the following questions (as well as ones you think of yourself):*

❏ *Was the goal I failed to meet a reasonable one for me—and was it* mine? Something to consider: you're much more likely to succeed at something if it is your own idea, something you really want to do versus something someone else wants for you. If you're trying—and failing—to achieve someone else's goal for you, you might ask yourself whether what's happening is really failure— or simply a goal that's not quite right for you.

Another thought: even if the goal was your idea, was it reasonable? Many dreams worth having take a lot of time and practice to achieve. For example, you might be a very gifted singer, musician, dancer or athlete, but you need time, training and discipline to polish your natural talents and to win that talent contest, get that first professional job or make the varsity team. The most talented and well-trained entertainers or athletes make what they do look easy and natural, but behind that sense of ease you would find years of hard work and preparation—so if you expect to be an expert at something very quickly, think again. You're not a failure if you need time to polish your skills. It just means that you're normal and human like the rest of us.

❑ *Would your best friend say you're a failure? Or if you saw your best friend in exactly the same situation, would you label him or her a "failure"?* If you stop and think about it, you may be much kinder to your friends than you are to yourself. What might be an understandable mistake in a friend feels like a horrible disaster when you're the one responsible. Consider giving yourself a break and treating yourself at least as well as you treat your friends!

❑ *Do you overuse the word "failure"?* Are you the

kind of person who feels that if you don't do everything perfectly, if you're not in first place or even if you make a very human mistake, you're automatically a failure?

Keep in mind: a mistake is *not* a failure. (We often learn only by making mistakes.) Coming in second or third or not even placing at all is not a failure. What counts is that you made the effort, tried and took a risk. Not being popular in school or not having a date to the prom or not having a boyfriend or girlfriend can hurt a *lot* at this point in your life—but this doesn't mean that you're a failure. Sometimes the smartest, most interesting people are labeled "geeks" or "brains" and shunned by peers in junior high or high school. Sometimes people who are genuinely good, worthwhile and wonderful potential love partners are ignored by classmates because they're too shy or not blond or thin enough or too skinny or too short or just don't fit that particular school's profile of what it takes to be popular. Even if those solitary lunches or those nights sitting home alone seem endless now, it won't always be that way. Some people reach their peak in high school. Others find their times of greatest success and happiness in the years after high school. If your best of times is definitely not now, this doesn't make you a failure.

Don't forget: you don't need a boyfriend or girlfriend to be a worthwhile person. Your times alone can be growing times when you learn who you are and what you want out of life.

❏ *What is failing at a task or goal doing* for *you?*
Before you dismiss this as an incredibly dumb
question, stop and think: failing to meet a goal
or develop a skill can do a lot for you—like
alerting your parents to the fact that you really
hate piano lessons and have no interest in winning this or any other music competition, or
to the fact that you're feeling overloaded and
can't do everything perfectly. Or you may have
had a big interest—like dancing—when you
were younger, but now you'd really like to
quit . . . except you have friends in dance class
that you'd miss or you hate to let your dance
teacher down or you feel guilty when you think
about how much money your parents have spent
over the years on lessons . . . so you might sabotage yourself (maybe without realizing it) by
not practicing enough. It may be easier to communicate your lack of interest and commitment
via failure to progress than by saying "This
doesn't feel right for me anymore and I'd like to
quit!"

❏ *In what ways are you—and aren't you—responsible for this failure?* Keep in mind: we don't always fail through lack of effort or ability, but
circumstances can, at least temporarily, come between you and a goal. A family emergency, a
badly timed case of the flu or even a flat tire en
route might make you miss team tryouts or
cheerleader auditions. There may be only a few
votes—or even one vote—standing between you
and a class election—and the voting process isn't

always totally fair, especially when certain offices or activities at your school are ruled by certain cliques. So sometimes the failure is entirely out of your control—though it may be a major disappointment for you.

But also keep in mind: it's important to take responsibility for our own mistakes and failures when appropriate. Did you blow a final or set a record for embarrassingly awful PSAT, SAT or ACT scores? Instead of just blaming the test as biased, stupid or unfair, think of ways you might improve your test-taking skills or performance. In the same way, some teachers *are* unfair and just have it in for you, but it makes sense to think about what role you might have played in stirring your teacher's wrath and how you can work to improve the situation. When you take at least some responsibility (when appropriate) for a failure, you empower yourself to do better in the future.

❏ *What can you learn from this experience?* What looks like failure can be a learning experience. Maybe you have learned that you need to prepare yourself more thoroughly for an exam or tryout or job interview. Maybe you've learned that a certain goal or activity just isn't for you. Maybe you've learned that you can survive setbacks and disappointments better than you ever imagined you could. You always thought you'd die if you didn't make the team or have a date for an important event or get into your first-choice college. But the worst has happened, and while you're sad, disappointed and maybe angry as well, you didn't die and life will go on. That's an important lesson for dealing with life's rough spots. If you're heartbroken today, life won't necessarily be wonderful tomorrow or next week or even next month. Major hurts and disappointments may linger in your memory for a long time—even years. But the pain does tend to lessen with time and perspective. And what looks like a disaster today may look like a positive turning point in the future. For example, Nora had long dreamed of attending Northwestern University. She had a very strong record in terms of recommendations, her extracurricular activities and community service. She greatly impressed the admissions interviewer, getting a high score there. But her GPA was too far below Northwestern's minimum cutoff point and so she was denied admission. And it felt like a disaster when she held that rejection letter in her hand and tried to imagine herself at her second-choice college. Now, four years later, she smiles when she remembers that awful day. "Why didn't I know then what I know now—that my second-choice college was exactly the right place for me?" she says. Indeed, Nora has thrived in college, earning excellent grades and being elected student body president. She has just been accepted into a challenging graduate program that will prepare her for a career in college administration. "In some ways," Nora says, reflecting back on her big disappointment, "my life really began when I had to let go of my dream to attend Northwestern and get on with my life. Going to college in California instead turned out to be just right for me. I've gone from feeling like a failure to feeling on top of the world. It didn't happen right away, but what's important is that it happened. My life went on—and got even better!"

✓ *Be gentle with yourself.* Think of how you would treat a close friend who was feeling sad and disappointed— and then treat yourself the same way. This may mean not giving yourself a hard time—over and over again— about a mistake you made. It may mean doing things that please you: taking a long walk, listening to your favorite CD, enjoying a hot bath or long, steamy shower, talking with a friend on the phone, playing a (perhaps long neglected) musical instrument, reading or rereading an especially funny or uplifting book or watching a favorite video, romping or cuddling with your pet. Allowing gentle pleasures in your life, even during difficult times, will help you to heal and regain hope for the future and belief in yourself.

✓ *Let others know how you feel.* If you don't let others who care know how you're feeling, they might not be able to help you. Even those who love you most aren't mind readers. Especially if you act as if a disappointment doesn't matter (even though you're really hurting inside), you shut others out just when you need them most. It's important, too, to let others who may be adding to your feelings of failure know how their words are affecting you. Some parents who push their kids to succeed in ways that they themselves would have liked to but didn't may react to a teen's setback or failure to achieve a goal with anger and very obvious disappointment of their own. It's important to let them know that you need their support, not their criticism, right now. Even if they can't be as supportive as you need them to be, remember that their anger and disappointment may not be as much about you as about their own missed opportunities.

✓ *Devise an action plan.* Your own personal action plan may be to work harder, sharpen your skills and go after that missed goal once again. Or it might be letting go of that dream or that goal to make room for a new one in your life. It could mean finding an advocate to help you discover new strengths and talents and build new dreams.

HOW TO KNOW WHEN YOU NEED EXTRA HELP...

You may need extra help in getting past your sense of failure and building your self esteem if:

- A parent won't let go of a goal he or she has for you or if a parent or other family member persists in calling you a failure.
- ℞ *Find an adult friend or advocate who can help you.* This might be a trusted family member, an adult

friend, a teacher, coach or counselor who could talk with your parent on your behalf and/or help you to feel good about yourself even if a parent is disappointed in you.

• You just can't shake your feelings of depression and general failure, no matter what anyone close to you says or does.

℞ *Get counseling—either alone or with your family.* It doesn't necessarily have to last a long time or cost a lot, but it can go a long way toward helping you to see yourself and your experiences in a less limited and more positive way. Family therapy can help to improve your family relationships and communication so that all of you are better able to help one another in a crisis.

• You're feeling such a profound sense of failure that you feel hopeless—and are even thinking about suicide.

℞ *Reach out for help* immediately *(even if you feel it's pointless).* It may sound trite, but it is also very true that suicide is a permanent solution to a temporary problem. You need someone to help you see that as long as there is life there is hope. Deep down, you may not want to die, but to live differently. As impossible as that might seem right now, it can happen for you.

Where can you turn: in a crisis call your local suicide hot line. If you're feeling a crisis building, ask a parent or an adult friend or family member who can help you immediately.

Life can get better—if you allow time, your own inner strength and the love of others to help you heal and see new options for yourself. If you give yourself a chance to grow through your pain, and others a chance to help, you may come to realize that, whatever mistakes you have made, you are a valuable, worthwhile person.

6

My Family Is Changing . . . and My Life Is Falling Apart

My life is falling apart. My parents got divorced recently and I hardly ever see Dad and Mom cries a lot and yells at me for nothing. We had to give up our house and move in with Grandma (who bugs me about every little thing) and I'm in a new school I totally hate. What's bad is that I wonder if this whole thing is my fault . . . like if I hadn't fussed and argued with my parents so much or if I had kept my room cleaner, maybe my dad wouldn't have left.

—Marta

My dad is getting remarried—just two months after my parents' divorce was final! I really, really hate his girl-friend and I also don't like the guy my mom is seeing now either. I feel like no one cares about me. *I'm just in the way. It's so stupid because my parents were more right for each other than they are with these new people. We were a pretty good family. How can I get them to see this??*

—Chris J.

I'm so miserable I don't know what to do. My parents divorced several years ago and both have remarried. My dad has a new baby girl and two stepsons and my stepfather has three brat-kids who are with us every other weekend and make my life total hell. I feel like running away, because no one notices me except to ask me to do something or to yell at me for not doing something or for sulking. How can I possibly be happy when my life is so horrible? I feel like getting stoned for the next ten years!

—Jana

The painful experience of a parental divorce can have a huge impact on you—more than many adults may realize. Some parents, in fact, choose to get divorced when their kids are teenagers because they believe that, as teens become more involved with friends than family, a divorce will hurt them less at that time. But that isn't necessarily the case.

In her study on children of divorce, Dr. Judith Wallerstein found that more than one-third of the children and teenagers were still moderately to severely depressed five to ten years after their parents' divorce.

Other studies have documented the pain of divorce and its impact on the lives of countless teenagers. For example, one recent study found that girls whose parents are divorced are at greater risk for early sexual activity and pregnancy as well as dropping out of school. Boys are at greater risk for dropping out of school and for aggressive behavior. And a 1992 study found that teens whose parents had divorced had higher levels of depression and lower self-esteem than their peers whose parents had not divorced.

This doesn't mean that if your parents divorce, your life is ruined and you're doomed to lingering depression, trouble in school and early pregnancy. It means that to avoid such painful aftershocks, you need to take care of yourself by dealing directly with your feelings and getting help when it all feels overwhelming.

If you're like most teenagers whose parents are divorced or divorcing, you may have a confusing array of feelings.

You may feel pain at watching the love between your parents fade and at losing your family as you've always known it. You may be wondering whether, if your parents can cease to love each other, they might also cease to love you.

You may feel guilty, wondering if you might have caused some of your parents' problems.

You may fear the future and what it might bring.

You may resent some of the changes in your life: less money, more responsibility, less time to yourself or less time with either parent, a move to a new home and/or new school and the loss of certain luxuries (that may feel like necessities to you), such as special lessons.

You may feel angry at your parents for not working their problems out in a way that would allow them to stay together, or for being so caught up in their own pain that they can't always see yours.

Or you may feel relieved that your parents have finally split and that the sullen silences, heated arguments and high tension your family experienced are no longer part of your life—at least not on a daily basis.

And you may be wondering if there's still a possibility that all this could be undone—and your parents could be happy together again. It can be very difficult to accept the reality of divorce and to give up those secret dreams of your family being reunited. There may be times when you hope against hope that your wishing for reunion will make it so.

Wishing rarely makes it so, however, and realizing that there are times in life when you don't have power over what happens can be especially scary and painful. You may feel a lot of fear, rage and grief before accepting the reality that your life as a family has changed forever.

HOW TO HELP YOURSELF WHEN YOUR FAMILY IS FALLING APART

✓ *Allow your feelings to happen—and accept them as normal.* It's entirely normal to feel sadness, rage, desperation, to want to wish the whole problem away and to have revenge fantasies ("I'll show them . . . They're messing up my life with this divorce. I'll *really* screw things up for myself and then they'll be sorry!") It's normal to have mixed feelings toward someone you love who has hurt you, even without meaning to. For example, you may feel love, longing and rage that feels like hatred for the parent who left, or anger mixed with compassion for the parent who was left, as you wonder if he or she could have tried harder or been a better spouse and avoided all this family misery. The fact is, feelings can't be judged. They just happen. What matters is what you *do* with these feelings.

Angrily blaming your parents for ruining your life, telling the parent who has left that you hate him or her and never want to see him/her again or taking your anger out on the parent you live with can only add to the general misery. So can allowing your pain to interfere with your friendships (just when you need your friends the most!) or your school work or your personal choices.

On the other hand, accepting and admitting painful feelings, discussing these with trusted friends or relatives, or in a group for teens whose parents are divorced, or with a counselor, can help you grow through your pain to new inner peace and hope, no matter how unpromising life seems to be at the moment.

✓ *Don't blame yourself for your parents' divorce.* Especially if the thought of being powerless to change anything scares you, it may be easy to fall into blaming yourself for your parents' marital troubles. Even if your parents *say* you've driven them to divorce, that's pretty unlikely. A strong, loving marriage can survive many family storms and stresses. Parental arguments may seem always to center on you (that often happens in a troubled family); parents who have difficulties with each other will often focus on conflict over a child even though this particular conflict may be a small part of their difficulties together. Expressing anger over or through a child they both love may feel safer to them than addressing the sadness, rage and disappointment they feel toward each other. Your parents are fighting and breaking up for their *own* reasons—most of which have nothing to do with you.

Realizing that your parents' crisis is not your fault can be both scary and liberating: it can be scary in the sense that you realize that there is nothing you can do to change what's happening between your parents. At the same time, this realization can free you to rise above these tensions and find your own ways of dealing with your changing life.

✓ *Don't allow yourself to be caught between your parents.* Some parents, in their post-divorce anger, unhappiness and discomfort with each other, use their children as messengers and sometimes even as unwitting spies. If your parents are constantly asking you to carry messages to each other or are quizzing you relentlessly about each other, it's time to call a halt—with respect and with love. It's important to remember that when your parents use you in this way, they probably aren't trying to hurt you. They're just not thinking clearly, because of their own pain. It may be up to you to tell them how *you* feel about what they're asking of you and why you need to say no. The basic message your parents need to hear is "I feel uncomfortable being a messenger or a spy. I would like the freedom to spend time with and love you both."

✓ *Give your newly blended family time to feel comfortable with (or tolerate) one another.* Perhaps your discomfort is a matter of not agreeing with your parent's choice of new partner. Not only is this person invading your family, but he or she is also . . . just totally unacceptable—not someone you'd spend five minutes with under other circumstances.

If this sounds familiar, remember that your parents are separate from you. Their choices do not reflect on you. It may help to concentrate on your own friends and your own life as much as possible, all the while being polite to your family's newcomer(s). You may find, in time, that after the new spouse or new stepsiblings have been around for a while, they're not quite as annoying. A parental remarriage is a big adjustment for you—and for everyone else in the family. You may feel a loss of privacy, a loss of attention from your parent and a lot more responsibility around the house if the remarriage has brought new and younger stepsiblings and/or a new baby half-brother or -sister. The latter can be a shock, especially if you've been an only child or the only child of a particular gender until now. You may wonder, at times, if there is enough love and nurturing to go around.

If your family is like most, there may *not* be enough now as everyone is trying to adjust to a new marriage and a newly blended family. This is a time to reach out to extended family members—grandparents, aunts, uncles, cousins, family friends—to fill in the gap.

Family meetings can also help during this time of adjustment—especially if some family members are feeling unfairly burdened or if there is a lot of jealousy between stepsiblings or between kids and a stepparent. Talking about what's happening and how you're feeling and working out some solutions together can go a long way toward building some tolerance and order out of the chaos, if not love and goodwill.

Keep in mind that comfort and good feelings take time to develop—not just weeks or months but sometimes even several *years*. So if it has been six months and you're still feeling that you have a stranger or strangers in your house and your life and it's not feeling right . . . you're not at all unusual. Time and growing tolerance may help. You may or may not come to love one another, but you *can* learn to tolerate one another.

In time, you may be pleasantly surprised by your new family members. Especially if you keep in mind that your own parents are not perfect, so it's unfair to expect a new stepparent to be perfect, and keep your mind open for positive qualities that person may have. You may make some joyous discoveries.

✓ *Beware of looking for love and attention in ways and places that could be harmful to you.* Especially when you're feeling abandoned by remarried parents or parents who are so caught up in their own social lives that there doesn't seem to be much love and attention leftover to give you, it can be tempting to look to romantic and/or sexual relationships of your own to fill this gap. But a boyfriend or girlfriend can't really be a parent to you, can't make up to you for the loss of parental affection and attention. In the same way, having sex (even with someone you love) can only distract you from your pain and loneliness for a little while—if at all. It's a risky non-solution. As uncomfortable as it may feel for you, you need to face your feelings of abandonment, loneliness, anger and sadness and look to your parents—perhaps with the help of another family member—for the love you're missing. Doing this will also help your romantic love relationship(s) because you will be able to start seeing your partner as he or she is, not as someone you're casting in the role of substitute parent. When you free your boyfriend or girlfriend of that emotional burden, you free the relationship to grow in healthy and happy ways.

✓ *Seek special support from people who* really *understand.* It can be immensely reassuring to talk with friends who have also experienced a parental divorce, or even to join a support group for teens whose parents are divorced or in the process of divorce. The more you talk with and listen to others, the more you'll realize that you're not alone.

✓ *Consider any positive impact these changes have had on you and your life.* When you're shocked and hurting, it may seem impossible to imagine anything positive about your parents divorcing. In time, not even the absence of daily conflict (if that was what home was like just before your parents split up) may be reassuring. You may need to look within yourself for positive aspects. Maybe you're stronger than you ever imagined you could be. Maybe you're feeling more competent and independent than most people your age. Maybe you feel newly reassured that your parents can lose their love for each other while still loving you, or that if one parent really doesn't seem to love you anymore, this doesn't mean that you're inherently unlovable. All of these realizations can contribute to your personal growth in many ways.

Jim, sixteen, says that his parents' divorce "made me grow up a lot. I realized that I couldn't always have my way and that my parents are people with their own lives. Before, I had seen them only as *my parents.* Now I can see and appreciate them in new ways. When I began to see them as human, it made it easier for me to feel independent from them and, at the same time, to care a lot for them, too."

Diana, fifteen, observes that "I used to be pretty help-less like a lot of my friends, but now I've learned to cook, shop, budget and make lots of decisions on my own. I've done a lot of thinking, too, about how I want my life to be. I don't ever want to be in my mom's spot: divorced with three kids, no work skills or experience and working at a boring, low-paying job. I want to go to college and have a career whether or not I get married. I don't think I'll get married right out of school like my parents did. I'd like to have a life of my own and be able to take care of myself whatever happens. I don't ever want to feel as powerless as my mom feels—and is. When I do get married, and stay married, it will be for love and a family, not for financial support. I mean, it just makes sense. But my parents' divorce put a lot of sense into my head where there were just dreams and fantasies before."

HOW TO KNOW IF YOU NEED EXTRA HELP...

You may need extra help in coping with your parental divorce or remarriage crisis if:

- Your sadness is interfering with your life in sig-nificant ways long after the divorce and remar-riage.
- You're being abused—verbally, physically or sex-ually—by a stepparent or parental boyfriend or girlfriend.
- You're feeling out of control, angry or are even

having fantasies of violence toward a new half-sibling or stepsibling.

• Despite your best efforts, the family adjustment and tolerance isn't happening and you feel stuck in a painfully chaotic family situation.

℞ *Get professional help for yourself or for your family.* This might be easiest if you seek help from an adult you know well who also has knowledge of mental health resources in your community: a school counselor or teacher, your pastor or church youth group leader or your family physician. This person may be able to offer you much-needed support, a good referral to a counseling professional and, not so incidentally, may be able to help convince your parent or parents to utilize this source of help.

Please note: if you are being abused, any professional you tell—and this can include teachers and school counselors as well as physicians and mental health professionals—may be legally obligated to report the abuse to a special children's protective services agency. As frightening as this prospect may seem, it can be the first step in changing your painful and dangerous life situation if you are, in fact, being abused. (If you are not and just feel tempted to say so to get back at a hated stepparent, keep in mind that there are much better ways to remedy your situation.)

A good family counselor, social worker, psychologist or psychiatrist (these are all mental health professionals) may be able to work with you and your family to alleviate conflicts, bring both negative and positive feelings into the open and help improve understanding, tolerance and love within your family.

Living through the crisis of a parental divorce can make you wonder, for a time, if you'll ever be able to love or trust another person, or whether you'll ever be happy again.

While some people may live lives scarred by pain and bitterness, others survive the worst possible home situations to live happy, normal adult lives. You can, too. Your attitude about your present crisis can have a big impact on your life in the years to come.

To free yourself from pain and bitterness, you need to realize that some things are truly beyond your control, that your parents' problems are *not* yours, and finally, you need to forgive your parents for not being perfect and for not being able to stay together. When you're in pain and enraged at one or both parents, such forgiveness may seem impossible. Instead, you may feel an urge to strike back at your parents and to hurt them as they have hurt you.

Unfortunately, this revenge can hurt you the most, keeping you tied to a painful situation for years—even after it has ceased to exist! Some people, quite needlessly, lead bitter, unhappy lives, sometimes sabotaging their own goals and dreams to get back at their parents for long-ago problems. They only succeed in perpetuating their own pain.

Remember that blaming ties you to the past. Revenge can hold you back from doing what you really want and need to do. In order to grow and go on, you must let go of your past and forgive.

"It's important to see your parents as people who have made mistakes like anyone else," says Dr. Doris Lion, a psychotherapist in Encino, California. "Sometimes their mistakes hurt you. Instead of being bitter, tell yourself that your parents are doing or have done the best they could. Then let it go."

Forgiving does not mean denying or minimizing what happened or saying they were right, but it will eventually free you to find your own ways to be happy. You may always feel some hurt, but forgiving your parents sets you free to value yourself, and free to reach out to others, free to trust and free to love.

7

I'm Having a Sexuality-Related Crisis— Date Rape, Sexually Transmitted Disease, Pregnancy— and I Don't Know What to Do!

Please help me. I'm desperate! I've been going with this guy at school who's really popular because he's our best football player. All the girls want to go out with him and I was really excited when he invited me to the Homecoming dance. But afterwards, in the car, we parked, had a few beers and then he attacked me and forced me to have sex with him. It wasn't at all like he even cared about me as a person. I'm so upset, I can't tell anyone and I can't face going to school tomorrow. If I told my parents, they'd kill me for parking and drinking with him. What can I do? If he is mean at school or just ignores me as if nothing happened, I don't know what I'll do. Help!

—Ashleigh

I have this discharge that's really irritating and feel pain inside me, too. I've been having sex, but only with one person. This couldn't be some sort of problem caused by sex—or could it?

—Chrystal H.

Can you get pregnant if you've only had sex a few times? What if your boyfriend pulls out? My boyfriend did that and we haven't had sex that much, like only three times before he went into the Army down in Texas. But I've missed two periods, have been really tired and threw up twice yesterday. Do you think I'm pregnant? I'm scared to get one of those store kits that would tell me for sure because I don't know what I'll do if I am pregnant. My boyfriend doesn't want to get married until I'm eighteen and right now I'm only fifteen. What should I do?

—Mandi L.

You may feel very lonely when you're in the middle of a sexuality-related crisis, but you're far from alone. It is estimated that every day in the United States about three thousand teenage girls get pregnant, and this results in about one million babies born to teenage mothers each year. Some 2.5 million teenagers a year are infected with a sexually transmitted disease. And date or acquaintance rape is an increasingly common and serious problem on high school and college campuses across the United States.

What can you do to prevent or to cope with a sexuality-related crisis?

DATE/ACQUAINTANCE RAPE

This kind of sexual assault is what Ashleigh described in her letter. Sexual assault can include forced sexual intercourse by use or threat of force, sexual abuse without penetration, attempted rape or sexual intimidation.

Who is at greatest risk? Recent studies have found that women most at risk include those who:

- Are college freshmen or high school students
- Date athletes or men who belong to fraternities
- Drink on dates

A study at a large midwestern university found, for example, that while only 2 percent of men on campus were athletes and only 25 percent belonged to fraternities, fraternity men accounted for 47.6 percent of sexual assaults on campus, and 20.2 percent of male perpetrators of sexual assault were athletes. The study also found that 82.7 percent of the women involved were assaulted by someone they knew and that 55 percent of the women and nearly 68 percent of the men had been drinking at the time.

Prevention Tactics

✓ *Think twice about mixing alcohol and dating.* This doesn't mean being banished to total geekdom or that you can't go to parties or have a good time. It simply means that in order to stay in control of your own body and destiny, you might give some thought to staying sober and, ideally, choosing to be with people who know how to have a good time without getting drunk.

✓ *Avoid situations that spell "trouble."* Especially if you're a high school student, going to a fraternity party, especially one where liquor will be flowing freely, is *not* a smart idea. It is also not a good idea to go to a guy's dorm room or his bedroom at home, especially if his parents aren't home. This is all particularly true if you know the guy but have only gone out with him a few times or if either of you has been drinking.

A good rule of thumb: if the thought occurs to you "My parents would just *kill* me if they knew I was here!" think twice about being there in the first place.

✓ *Set firm boundaries.* This doesn't mean making "Don't touch me!" your most frequently uttered expression or becoming a total dork no one wants to go out with. It means letting the people you date know that when you say no you *mean* no. It means being very clear about what you will and won't do. This, of course, applies to both sexes—and men have as much right as women to say no.

What to Do When You Are a Victim of Date/ Acquaintance Rape

Why you need immediate professional help: If you are planning to press charges against the person who raped you, physical evidence must be documented. Having a medical examination at an emergency room or clinic can ascertain whether semen is present in your vagina and whether there are bruises and other physical signs of force. Even if you don't press charges, you still need medical help: tests for STD, an HIV test now (and a follow-up HIV test six months from now), a "Morning After" pill to prevent pregnancy, other physical treatment as needed and crisis counseling.

✓ *Tell adults and friends who can help you.* You may be so hurt, so devastated, so in shock that it's hard to know what to do. Tell someone who can help you to get immediate medical attention and give you emotional support in those first hours or days after the attack.

✓ *Express your feelings about what happened in ways that are helpful to you.* You may have a confusing array of feelings—anger, fear, depression, deep humiliation and shattered faith in others. You may also be shocked when some friends try to blame you for the assault (saying you should have been more careful or that you must not have said no firmly enough) or shrug off the incident as a matter of "boys being boys." It can be tempting to withdraw from others, to get caught in your depression and anger, to secretly wonder if you were, indeed, at fault and to punish yourself. But all of that can only prolong the pain. Talk with people you trust about how you feel. Let your assailant know how you feel about what he did. Perhaps write a letter to him. You might mail it. You might not. But what matters is getting those feelings out and acknowledged so that you can resolve the pain and begin to get on with your life.

✓ *Get professional emotional support.* Call your local rape crisis line for immediate help and later referral to a therapist who can help you deal with your feelings over time.

✓ *If you plan to bring legal charges against your assailant, think about bringing the matter to civil rather than criminal court.* This is the advice of Dr. Andrea Parrott of Cornell University, who points out that the criminal court's judgment may not be very satisfying and that a civil court is more likely to decide in your favor. She says that you may be able to sue a third party—such as a fraternity or a school—for damages and the cost of psychotherapy if inadequate security was a component of your assault.

SEXUALLY TRANSMITTED DISEASES

Your first clue may be an unusual or uncomfortable discharge, a painful or painless growth or rash in or around your genital area. Or it may be evidence—like itching—of a parasitic sexually transmitted disease. Or you may simply have had unplanned and unprotected sex or other intimate contact with another and now are worried about getting a sexually transmitted disease.

The basic fact you need to know about sexually transmitted diseases is that if you are having sex or close, genital contact with another person or persons, you are running the risk of getting sexually transmitted diseases. Nice people get STDs. Even if you've had or are having sex with only one person in your life, you risk getting an STD if that other person was infected by a previous partner or is not as faithful as you are in the relationship.

Prevention Tactics
✓ *Abstinence.* By abstaining from sexual intercourse and other risky activities—like heavy petting and oral sex—until you are married and/or in a mutually monogamous relationship, you can decrease your chances

of ever getting a sexually transmitted disease. This option isn't for everybody, but it is the surest way we know to take yourself out of the STD risk category.

✓ *Be selective about your partners.* While you can't tell by just looking at a person whether or not he or she may be infected with a sexually transmitted disease, selectivity is one way you can decrease your risk of getting an STD if you are sexually active. The fact is, the more sexual partners you have, the greater your risk of infection. In this day of AIDS and other life or fertility-threatening sexually transmitted diseases, this is no small consideration. The diseases *can* happen to you! So be careful. Don't have sex with relative strangers, with people known to sleep around a lot, with people you know or suspect may be IV drug users. Ideally, a partner should be someone you know and trust enough to discuss sexual histories with, and someone to whom you can say "For our own protection, we need to use a condom" without undue embarrassment.

✓ *Use condoms every time you have sex.* That is a must whether you are gay or straight. While some teens complain that these get expensive after a while, think about it: condoms are a lot less expensive than dealing with the medical consequences of a sexually transmitted disease or, not so incidentally, with the expense of an unplanned pregnancy and parenthood.

At the same time, you need to be aware that while using condoms can give you some protection against diseases like AIDS, gonorrhea, chlamydia and syphilis, the protection may not be 100 percent if the condom is not used correctly or if it tears or breaks. Also, you need to know that condoms cannot completely protect you against some forms of STDs, such as herpes, genital warts or pubic lice.

What to Do if You Think You May Have a Sexually Transmitted Disease

Why you need immediate medical help: Sexually transmitted diseases do *not* ever just go away by themselves without medical intervention. Prompt medical help will prevent even greater discomfort and health- or life-threatening consequences. For example, chlamydia, which is the most common STD in the United States today, if left untreated can cause serious pelvic or cervical infections in women and inflammation of the sperm-carrying passage in men, putting those infected at risk of infertility. Pelvic inflammatory disease can also be a serious health threat for women. Untreated gonorrhea can damage joints and heart valves. And the virus causing genital warts has also been linked to cervical cancer in women. It is estimated that 10 to 15 percent of women with untreated genital warts develop cervical cancer. Another good reason for early treatment: you can get cured and/or counseled so that you will not spread your sexually transmitted disease on to a future partner.

✓ *Don't be shy: get immediate medical help.* You will not be the first—or the last—person with a sexually transmitted disease that your doctor will see. Nevertheless, if you're too embarrassed to go to your regular doctor, go to your local health department clinic, youth clinic or teen clinic for evaluation and treatment.

An important note: you can get completely confidential medical treatment without parental consent if you are over the age of twelve and feel that you may have a sexually transmitted disease.

✓ *Let your partner know if you are diagnosed with a sexually transmitted disease.* This can be very difficult emotionally if your partner is the only person who could have given you the disease, if your partner has been faithful and you haven't or if this disease seems to have come out of nowhere to plague a mutually monogamous relationship.

In the latter case, it's important to know that STDs such as herpes may lie dormant for months, even years, and so could occur in a relationship where both partners are faithful to each other.

In any event, letting your partner or partners know—even if this is very difficult—is the decent thing to do. In many instances, such as in gonorrhea or chlamydia, men will have early symptoms, but women are not likely to have symptoms until the disease has spread to the pelvic region, with much more serious consequences. An early warning, then, can save a woman's fertility and perhaps even her health as well.

PREGNANCY

"But I never thought it could happen to me!"

When we think of how many times we have heard those words—uttered in astonishment and anguish—we feel sad and frustrated all over again. Of course, there is something truly miraculous about creating a new life, and whenever a pregnancy happens, it seems a bit unbelievable at first. But looking beyond the miraculous aspects of pregnancy and birth, there is one fact: if you are having sex (or are engaging in heavy petting where there is a possibility that semen could get into your vagina) you *can* get pregnant. Believe it.

You can get pregnant the first time you have sex.

You can get pregnant whether or not you enjoy sex, whatever position you use and whether or not you consciously *want* to get pregnant.

You are at risk for pregnancy *any* day of the month. Teens often have irregular menstrual cycles, making the most (or least) likely days for conception difficult to predict. It's safest to assume that pregnancy is possible whenever you have sex. Half of all teen pregnancies occur within the first six months after initial intercourse. Twenty percent of teenage girls get pregnant the first *month* they have sex. So, if you're having unprotected sex, it's quite likely that you will get pregnant eventually.

Pregnancy and early parenthood is life-changing. Becoming a parent before you have completed your education and have a reasonable degree of economic independence and security can put you at risk for lifelong poverty and unemployment. Having the sometimes overwhelming responsibility of parenting the next generation before you have completely grown up and experienced the fulfillment of some of your own hopes and dreams can lead to frustration, resentment and, in some instances, overinvestment in your child doing what you could not.

Parenthood is a pivotal role in anyone's life and is far

too important to be taken on because of a whim, romantic fantasies about having a baby with someone you love or simply chance.

Prevention Tactics

✓ *Dream your own dreams—and make these a priority in your life.* Study after study has shown that girls who have hopes and dreams for their own futures—whether these dreams are for college and career, travel or simply the freedom of independent living, working and socializing—tend not to get pregnant. It is when you can't really see a future for yourself that you think "Why not?" to early parenthood, to give your life meaning and focus.

We don't mean to diminish the importance of parenthood. It is one of the most important—if not *the* most important—life role you can play. But when you have a child, there are many instances where the needs of that child must come first. It is much easier to put your child's needs first when you have previously met many of your own. If you've always wanted to run off to Hawaii with your best friend, share an apartment, work and enjoy life in the tropics, make concrete plans to do just that: getting in-demand work skills so that you can get a job anywhere, planning and saving money for a tropical adventure that will give you memories for a lifetime. If you have dreams of becoming a veterinarian, go for it—knowing that this means doing well in high school *and* in college so that you can be admitted to a veterinary medicine school. When you have a dream for your future, it takes hard work and planning to achieve it—and that may mean postponing other life events and choices, like parenthood.

You may be a much happier, more giving parent if you have given yourself the gift of going after your own dreams first. Then you can help and encourage your children to do the same.

✓ *Consider postponing sexual activity.* Abstinence is the only 100 percent effective form of birth control (though some methods such as birth control pills come close if used consistently and correctly). Choosing to postpone sex until marriage or until you have completed your education and have achieved economic and emotional independence is not necessarily easy, but it can be a very positive choice in terms of helping you to avoid the risks of pregnancy while you work to finish school and get established on your own.

✓ *Learn about and* use *reliable methods of birth control.* If you do decide to have sex, see a physician and get help with determining the best form of birth control for you. While condoms used with spermicidal jelly are an essential protection against AIDS infection and are therefore ideally used by all couples who are having sex, some women also choose to take birth control pills or use another form of contraception for added protection against pregnancy.

If the thought of going to your family doctor for birth control seems too expensive or embarrassing a prospect, call your local Planned Parenthood clinic for low- or no-cost help on a confidential basis.

Something to remember: the most reliable form of birth control won't work unless you use it correctly and consistently. And if you're embarrassed to even *think* about birth control, let alone talk about it with a partner or your doctor, think about this: birth control isn't nearly as embarrassing to deal with or as troublesome as an unplanned pregnancy would be. If you're having sex—or thinking about having sex—you need a reliable method of birth control *now!*

✓ *Get real about parenting.* If you're in love and thinking how cool it would be to have a baby together . . . if you're feeling lonely and without any special goals for the future, and are thinking how great it would be to have a baby to love who would love you back . . . if you love baby-sitting and just keep thinking how you would like, more than anything, a baby of your own—keep in mind that these feelings of wanting to share love with another and nurture a child of your own are normal, but you need to give considerable thought to the realities of parenting.

Being a parent is an incredibly demanding as well as joyous experience. It is a lifelong—not just an eighteen-year—commitment, as most parents will tell you. It can be a responsibility far beyond mere caretaking, as you nurture a cute but helpless baby, a demanding toddler, a needy child and a challenging teenager. Although there are many wonderful single parents, ideally—because parenting is so demanding—parenthood is shared by two people who are completely committed to the child's needs and to each other. Movie and TV stars may make single parenthood look glamorous, but it can be lonely, exhausting and very difficult to manage financially for the average person, especially if he or she has not finished high school, is unemployed (or employed at a low-paying job) and has little, if any, family support.

While good parents come in all ages and circumstances, in order to give you and your future children the best chance of being a healthy and happy family, think about giving yourself a chance to be young first, to do fun things, to finish school, to get established and to build a stable and secure relationship with another person before you become a parent.

What to Do if You Are (or Think You May Be) Pregnant

Why you need immediate medical help: Getting an early diagnosis of pregnancy and early prenatal care can be essential for several reasons. First, if you are thinking about abortion as an alternative, you need to pursue this possibility early in your pregnancy. Most abortions are performed in the first ten weeks of pregnancy. In fact, after the first ten to twelve weeks, it may be difficult, if not impossible, to get an abortion in some areas. If you are planning to have your baby and keep it or, perhaps, give it up for adoption, it's essential to safeguard your baby's health and development (the first three months are crucial) by getting medical help and advice and practicing good health habits, such as eating a balanced diet and not drinking or smoking or using drugs.

✓ *See a doctor immediately.* This is as much for your child's sake as your own. You may have figured out the diagnosis of pregnancy on your own—either via an over-the-counter testing kit or by noting a growing array of symptoms, such as missed period(s), nausea, fatigue or breast swelling and tenderness. Why should you go to a doctor then? In order to get absolute confirmation of your pregnancy, to review your options and, if you're choosing to continue the pregnancy, to get expert advice on what you need to do *now* to make sure your baby is born healthy.

✓ *Tell your parents or a trusted adult* now. This is more than you can handle alone, no matter how competent you are. You might think your parents will kill you—and they *may,* at least initially, be somewhat less than delighted at the news. But many parents surprise their teens by their loving supportiveness in a crisis—and you need that support now. If you know for a fact that your parents are in the minority who cannot and will not be supportive, try talking with a trusted adult friend and/ or a medical professional or counselor as you review your options. Your friends can offer a lot of support, of course, but most of them have not been in your place. It's easy to be very opinionated about abortion or about adoption as options, for example, or to extol the wonders of single parenting if you have not been in the position of being pregnant and knowing that any choice you make will have an impact on the rest of your life. An adult who has been there and who is a parent can help most of all with some perspective about the delights and the demands of parenting.

✓ *Realize that there are no perfect options, but one may be the most right (or least wrong) for you.* When you're trying to decide what to do, it's important to know that there is no one always-right solution, no perfect choice, as you review your options, from abortion to marrying the father, from adoption to single parenthood.

When considering abortion, keep in mind that this may be your best alternative only if *you* see it as your free and preferred choice. If abortion violates your personal ethical or religious beliefs, it may well not be for you, no matter how much sense it makes to someone else.

When considering marriage, keep in mind that a baby can put a strain on even the most mature and stable relationship. Some questions to ask yourself: would you marry him anyway eventually, even if you weren't pregnant? Are you—and is he—ready for the responsibility of marriage and parenthood? Do you have the support of your families? If you answer 'no' to any of the above, think twice before choosing this option.

When considering adoption, keep in mind that this can be a very loving, unselfish, though immensely painful option. It may help to remember that not all adoptions are closed (you never know what became of your child) these days. Some private, open adoptions may allow you to know and have some say about who adopts your child, and to be able to get information about and maybe, in some cases, even be in touch with the adoptive family as the child is growing up. Speak with agencies and with an attorney specializing in private adoptions as you review this possibility.

When considering keeping and raising the baby yourself, keep in mind that you're taking on the challenge of your life. Explore ways that you can care for your baby and yet stay in school and prepare, eventually, for a job or career that will enable you to support yourself and your child. Discuss with your parents or extended family the possibilities and the limits of their ability to help you. Don't just assume, for example, that your mom, who stayed home with you and your siblings and who has just recently started a career she truly enjoys, will automatically want to give it all up to stay home and care for your baby. Don't assume that you and your baby can count on indefinite parental support. Your parents may have life goals of their own, including other children to put through college, saving for retirement and having a little time and money to do some traveling on their own after long years of parental responsibility. If you will be relying on your family for all manner of support, this needs to be a *family* decision. And if you can't count on family support, you need to explore your options with a professional counselor to find the best resources for you and your baby.

As you can see, the options and solutions to sexuality-related crises are mostly imperfect, often difficult, but do-able with good medical help and counseling and the support of those you love as you review your options.

And the best option of all, in these instances, is prevention. Taking precautions to help prevent a rape or a sexually transmitted disease or an unplanned pregnancy is one of the best things you can possibly do for yourself.

8

I'm Gay/Lesbian and . . .

I feel so different from my friends and wonder why I have these feelings instead of liking girls like all the other guys in my class do.

—J.D.

I'm scared that my friends will hate me if they find out that I'm gay.

—G.W.

I'm lonely because I feel I can't let anyone know who I really am.

—H.J.

I'm angry that people make judgments when all I want to do is love and live a regular life.

—E.C.

I'm happy and sad . . . happy in love and sad because it has to be a secret.

—C.P.

I feel that no one will ever accept or understand me because I'm gay and wonder if I'll ever find someone special to love who will love me back . . .

—J.M.

The voices of gay and lesbian teens express a myriad of feelings, longings and life experiences. Some realize their sexual orientation early and grow up with a firm and positive sense of themselves as gay or lesbian. Others feel confused, wondering what it means when you're attracted to someone of the same sex: *is* it a phase or is it for life? Still others live in fear that they will be rejected by friends and family if they let people know their true feelings. Many people—gay and heterosexual—are confused about what it means to be gay: why people are gay or heterosexual and how to live a happy, productive life in a society that still is, to a large extent, homophobic.

WHAT DOES IT MEAN TO BE GAY OR LESBIAN?

We used to believe that a homosexual (gay or lesbian) was someone who, *as an adult,* felt a primary sexual preference for those of his or her own sex. This definition was careful to leave out teens who had erotic experiences with same-sex friends or crushes on those of the same sex. That was seen as a phase that was experimental and unlikely to last to adulthood.

Now we know that isn't always so.

It is true that many teens have erotic feelings and experiences of all kinds as they explore who they really are, and having crushes on those of the same or opposite sex is a normal part of growing up. But our thinking about teens and sexual orientation has changed a bit in the past few years.

Recent studies reveal that, while some young people may be in their late teens or early adulthood before they discover and accept their sexual orientation, a significant number of others know quite early in life that their sexual orientation is gay or lesbian.

Many teens we've seen report that they knew they were different in some way and that they were primarily attracted to those of their own sex as early as the age of five or six. Still others were quite certain who they were by the time they were in junior high.

In a recent Minnesota study of 34,706 teens in grades seven through twelve in that state, it was found that awareness of sexual identity evolves through adolescence, with most teenagers knowing their sexual orientation by the time they reached seventeen or eighteen. "At age twelve, 26 percent of the adolescents were unsure of their sexual orientation," reported primary researcher Dr. Gary Remafedi, of the Adolescent Health Program at the University of Minnesota. "Only 5 percent were still unsure of their sexual orientation by the age of seventeen."

For some, this journey to self-discovery begins with feelings of being different that are hard to pinpoint. Gradually, perhaps, feelings of attraction for the same sex become apparent. This doesn't mean that a person might not be attracted to the opposite sex as well and have experiences with them while being primarily attracted to those of the same sex.

For many people, sexual orientation is not strictly one extreme or the other. There are people, of course, who cannot respond emotionally or physically to those of the opposite *or* of the same sex. But these are extremes. Most people—both gay and heterosexual—fall somewhere in between.

There are gay people who have sexual feelings and experiences only with a partner or partners of their own sex but have very warm and enduring friendships with people of the opposite sex. The converse may be true of heterosexual people.

There are some gay people who have had sexual experiences with those of the opposite sex. Some have even married and had children.

And some heterosexuals have had some homosexual experiences—quite often in their teen years—but identify themselves as straight.

So while you may see yourself as primarily homosexual or heterosexual, putting strict labels on yourself can be confusing when your feelings or actions don't always match what society believes to be true of gays or straights. As human beings, we're capable of loving and finding beauty in many different kinds of people even though our primary sexual feelings may be focused on one gender or the other.

What causes an estimated 2 to 10 percent of the population to have primarily a homosexual orientation?

There is a lot of ongoing research that is looking into a complex mix of genetic, hormonal and environmental factors that may play a major part in determining sexual orientation.

Studies have looked at identical twins and other siblings to see if homosexuality might run in families, and others have addressed the question "Is homosexuality an inborn trait or is it learned behavior?" In all these studies, there have been some interesting findings. For example:

- Researchers at Boston and Northwestern universities have conducted joint studies of gay and lesbian people and their brothers and sisters. The findings: 52 percent of the identical twin brothers of gay men and 48 percent of the identical twin sisters of lesbian women were also homosexual; 22 percent of nonidentical twin brothers and sisters or other biological siblings of gay men and 16 percent of the same in lesbian women shared their sexual orientation; 10 percent of the adopted brothers of gay men and 6 percent of the adopted sisters of lesbian women were also gay or lesbian. These findings indicated that there may well be a genetic link to sexual orientation, since identical twins share the same genetic makeup and fraternal twins and other siblings have some similar genes. Now these researchers are looking at the identical twins who do not share the same sexual orientation to find out what other factors might have had an impact.

- Studies by former Salk Institute Researcher Dr. Simon LeVay and another study by Dr. Laura Allen and Dr. Roger Gorski at UCLA have found various differences in the brain structure between gay and heterosexual men.

Much research needs to be done, but the prevailing thought these days is that sexual orientation is *not* a choice or preference, but an intrinsic part of who you are. The factors that influence sexual orientation—whether gay or straight—seem to be a complex mix of genetic, hormonal and environmental influences that we don't totally understand.

We *are* beginning to understand many things that homosexuality is *not*, however. Homosexuality is *not* a disease or an aberration. It is *not* a choice or conscious preference. It is not, by definition, a problem. What can make homosexuality a problem for some people is the fear, ignorance, prejudice and discrimination surrounding gay and lesbian people in our society.

WHAT IT MEANS TO BE A GAY OR LESBIAN TEENAGER

Being a gay or lesbian teenager means being different from many of your peers at a time when it is very uncomfortable to be different.

Patrick, recalling his years as a high school football star who also had a 4.2 GPA and was voted "Male Student of the Year" in his graduating class before he went on to Harvard, thinks not of his many triumphs but of his deep loneliness and despair at that time in his life. "I was so lonely and so depressed about the fact that I was gay—and there was nothing I could do about it—that I constantly thought about killing myself throughout my senior year," he says.

Several years later, when he came out to family and close friends, Patrick got the love and acceptance he had hoped for—though not without tears.

Patrick's parents, even though loving and accepting, cried for hours that first night. They were afraid that he would get AIDS and die. They expressed their sorrow about the children he would not have, feeling as they did that he would have made a wonderful father. The tears gave way to hugs and expressions of unconditional love within days. But Patrick and his family are quick to point out that even the most loving family may take time to absorb and accept the fact that a son or daughter is gay, and that teens who fear revealing their sexual orientation to those they love most may have good reason to hesitate before letting others know about their sexuality. Being in the closet, however, can make one feel very frustrated, lonely and afraid of discovery.

Being a gay teenager may mean wondering "Why me?" while thinking how simple life would be as a heterosexual. There may be a temptation to pretend to be straight just because it's easier and is such a part of high school life: the obvious attractions, the dating, the proms. Everyone seems to be part of a couple, and everyone thinks that's just great as long as the couples are male and female.

In the past decade, a few gay and lesbian teens have taken a same-sex date to their high school proms, with mixed results and national headlines. In an effort to make this rite of passage more comfortable for gay and lesbian teens last year, the Los Angeles Unified School

District held an all-city prom at a Los Angeles hotel ballroom for gay and lesbian students. The event was considered a great success by students and organizers alike, even though the students attending had to cross a vocal picket line of demonstrators to get into the hotel, yet another reminder of the fact that some segments of our society do not accept—and may never accept—the fact that gay people are people like everyone else. While more people are tending to see being gay as an inborn trait—like having blue eyes or being left-handed—others view homosexuality as a moral issue and are quick to pass judgment.

So, yes, it can seem simpler at times to pretend that one is straight. It may be simpler, that is, for everyone but you as you grapple quietly with the pain of not being who you really are.

Being a gay or lesbian teenager is not necessarily a negative experience—despite the fears and feelings many have about being different from peers.

There may be the excitement of discovering who you really are, accepting and enjoying your uniqueness.

There may be that exquisite experience of falling in love for the first time.

There may be a firm conviction that you are proud to be the person you are—and that you will make a difference in the world. Making that difference may mean being the best you can be, reaching out a helping hand to other gay or lesbian people who are living in pain, confusion and frustration, or attempting to educate society, in your own way, that those who love people of their own gender are different only in that way.

WHAT TO DO IF YOU ARE OR FEEL YOU MIGHT BE GAY OR LESBIAN

✓ *Work on accepting your sexuality—whatever your orientation may be—as simply a part of who you are.* Keep in mind that we don't *choose* to be heterosexual or homosexual; sexual orientation seems to be an inborn trait. It is an important part of who you are, but only a *part.* Sexual orientation, like other traits, can't be judged. Sexual feelings can't be judged. These just happen. However, what you choose to *do* with your sexuality can be right or wrong. For example, it is wrong to exploit others sexually or to endanger your own health and that of others with unsafe sex practices—whatever your sexual orientation. But, deep down, you need to accept the fact that you are a good and lovable person whether you are gay or straight.

Accepting yourself in this way may prevent a lot of hurt and may even be life-saving. When you value who you are, you will not exploit others or allow yourself to be exploited. When you value who you are, you will be careful in choosing whether or not to have sex, and in consistently practicing safe sex. The teens we've encountered who don't do this—who don't insist on practicing safe sex, for example—often have such low self-esteem that they feel their lives are not worth protecting. When you value yourself, you feel that you have a right to stand up for yourself, for your own health, and to safeguard your own life.

Also, when you accept yourself—whether you are gay or straight—you will be more in tune with what is right for you in terms of sexual choices. Just as some straight people choose not to have sex until they are older or until they are married, some gay and lesbian people also take time to accept their feelings and themselves before becoming sexually involved with another. For example, even though Patrick, whom we mentioned earlier, realized that he was gay when he was still in high school, he did not have sex with anyone until he was in his early twenties. And Steve, 16, joined a support group for gay and lesbian teens in San Francisco about a year after he realized that he was gay. It was another year-and-a-half after joining the group before he had his first gay sexual experience. He waited, he told us, because "I wanted to feel good and secure about myself and because I was waiting for a good relationship with someone I loved. I didn't want to have just meaningless sex. That's not what I want to do. It's not what I want for myself."

When you value who you are, you will take great care to make choices that are positive and healthy ones for you.

✓ *Be selective about the people in whom you confide.* Being a self-accepting gay or lesbian person does not have to mean telling the world about your sexuality if you'd rather not. People have different needs for privacy, and if you'd rather keep your sexual orientation private—it's OK and entirely up to you.

Some people—both gay and heterosexual—choose to keep their love lives private, confiding only in close friends or family members.

Some people like to tell everyone they know when they are happy and in love.

Some gay people—angry at societal discrimination and proud to be different—are very "out" and sometimes act outrageously as well. That may or may not be your personal style.

Other gay people come out to those they know and love in stages: first, to people they strongly feel will understand and be supportive, and then to people who may have more negative reactions, at least initially.

"One of the first people I told was my friend Tony," says Joe. "We have been best friends for years—going hiking, camping and to an Outward Bound summer experience together. We were also debate team cochairmen. The only difference between us, really, is that Tony has a serious girlfriend. I was scared to tell Tony what I was feeling, but took a chance. He was surprised, but very supportive. A few weeks later, just before the sign-up deadline for a summer institute in debate at an Eastern college, he casually called to make sure I was going to get my application in on time so we could room together. After I confirmed our rooming arrangement, I hung up the phone and cried. I was so happy that my best friend still wanted to be my friend—like always."

Terri, who has known since she was in elementary school that she is attracted to women, says that she can talk fairly easily to close friends about being lesbian, but has yet to tell anyone in her family. "If my family rejected me, it would *really* hurt," she says. "Sometimes I think the word 'homophobia' should be spelled 'home-ophobia' and defined as fear of coming out at home."

So if you choose to go slowly and cautiously in revealing this aspect of your life to others, you have a lot of company and may be making a wise choice—for you.

✓ *If your family and friends react in a negative way to your revelation that you are gay, don't assume that it will always be that way.* Quite often, the people who love you most will need time to adjust to your news.

At first, they may question your conviction that you are gay: "How could you know? You're so young! It's just a phase. It will pass . . . if you just meet the right girl . . ." There may be tears as they express their feelings: fear that you will get AIDS and die at a young age; fear that you will never have a stable, rewarding lifetime love; sadness that you might not have children; fear that you will become a victim of discrimination.

Because your parents are likely to want only the best for you—the best opportunities, a long, healthy life, a loving family of your own—there may be times of tension and tears as they consider what it means to be gay in this society and readjust their dreams for you.

In time, they may come to realize that you are the same person you always were. They may come to realize that heterosexuality is no guarantee of lifetime love, that many gay and lesbian couples not only have lifelong relationships, but also raise children—biological or adopted—together. And not all gay men have or will get AIDS. (Celibacy, monogamy and safe sex are all options that are increasingly popular among homosexual as well as heterosexual young adults.)

These realizations may take time. While your parents, other family members or friends are in this process of working out their feelings about your revelation, keep in mind that this isn't likely to go on forever and that it isn't a sign that they don't love you. People who don't love you may be derisive or simply indifferent. People who love you *care*—and sometimes this caring is painful.

It may also help to keep in mind that *most* parents aren't thrilled to hear frank facts about their teenager's sexuality. That is often true no matter what your sexual orientation might be!

"When I was dating girls, my mom was having fits, fearing that I was having sex and would get the girl pregnant," Ben remembers. "Then, when I stopped dating girls and started spending time with Evan, she started worrying that I *wasn't* having sex with girls. Then she gradually came to realize that I was in love with Evan, and at first, it just blew her away. But she wouldn't have been really happy to hear anything about my sexuality. A lot of parents are like that. A lot of kids are, too. I mean, do you really want to think for more than ten seconds about your *parents* having sex? I think it all comes down to accepting one another as sexual beings, then giving one another the privacy and space to be ourselves."

Keep in mind that the same strong love that may be behind the tears and tensions now will bring all of you closer in the future as you understand and accept the ways you and those you love are different—as well as all the wonderful qualities, feelings and experiences that you share with one another.

✓ *Get support from others who know—and care—what it means to be a gay teenager or a family in a coming out crisis.* Many cities across the nation have teen support groups sponsored by local gay and lesbian centers. A number of high schools use the Project Ten material developed by Virginia Uribe of Fairfax High School in

Los Angeles to reach out to lonely, confused and fearful gay and lesbian teens.

Check your local telephone directory or dial the operator to connect with resources near you. Your physician or high school counselor, a teacher you trust or a local teen clinic may be able to refer you to special sources of help.

If you are or feel you may be gay or lesbian and are feeling in urgent need of help—maybe so depressed, desperate and lonely that you're thinking of taking your own life (gay teens have a two to three times greater suicide risk than their heterosexual peers)—here is a number you can call toll-free:

The Youth Crisis Hotline
1-800-448-4663

If your need is less urgent, but you just want to talk with someone who will understand how you feel, try the Gay and Lesbian Youth Talkline, which takes calls from 7 P.M. to 10 P.M. (PST) Monday through Saturday at (213) 993-7475.

These outside resources can be especially important if your parents or other family members continue to be unaccepting of you and of your sexual orientation.

If your family is struggling to come to terms with your sexual orientation, it may help to put your parents in touch with Parents and Friends of Lesbians and Gays, an organization that has more than two hundred chapters across the United States and additional groups in Canada and six other countries. You can find the chapter nearest you (and also get a list of publications that may be helpful) by writing to PFLAG Family and Chapter Support Office, P.O. Box 27606, Central Station, Washington, D.C. 20038.

DO NOT RUN AWAY!! No matter how tense things are, this is not the answer to your problems with your family. If you run away and try to live on the streets, you will be exposed to a myriad of dangers—including a greater chance of being exposed to the HIV virus that causes AIDS. You and your family can work things out in time. Try. It may take time, but it is well worth the effort.

✓ *Be open to counseling as a way of working through your own pain and anger.* This doesn't mean that being gay is, by definition, a problem, or that homosexual people need to get therapy automatically. (Sometimes family members will urge you to get therapy, hoping that this will somehow "fix what's wrong" with you.) Most reputable therapists today do not see homosexuality as an emotional problem or mental illness or defect to be "fixed." It's likely that a therapist would work with you to resolve your own painful feelings about being different or being rejected or criticized by your family and to help strengthen your good feelings about yourself.

Renee was in her first year of college when she met Jill, the love of her young life. Three years later, they are still together and happy in every way but one: Renee's family has let her know that if she is, in fact, a lesbian, she is no longer part of their family. So she feels caught between two worlds—wanting her parents' love and wanting a life with Jill. "There are nights I lie sleepless trying to figure out how to get my family to accept and love me for who I am," she says. "One of the most painful things in my life is knowing that my parents will never completely value or love me because of my sexual orientation. I've found the most wonderful person to share my life with, but if I shared that with my dad, he would never again acknowledge me as his daughter. I know that. And it is devastating." For Renee, the gentle support and affirmation she has received from a counselor at her student health center has been life-saving—and an inspiration for her future career. Renee is now preparing to become a psychologist and to work with young people much like herself.

You might find a therapist who is sensitive to gay issues via a referral from the hot line mentioned above or by a call to your local gay and lesbian center. Quite often, these services—ranging from individual therapy to special teen support groups—are available at low or no cost.

✓ *Be cautious about labeling yourself too quickly and too narrowly.* Don't rush to pin labels on yourself as the result of a crush on someone of the same sex or on the basis of one—or a few—sexual experiences with a same-sex partner. If you're not sure whether or not you are gay or lesbian, there's really no rush to put a label on your sexuality.

Live with and enjoy your feelings and your fantasies for a while without any pressure to act on these feelings anytime soon. Cultivate warm friendships among those of both sexes.

Keep in mind that your sexuality—including your sexual orientation—is an important part of who you are, but it is *only* a part. You also have other major discoveries to make about yourself—your talents, your strengths, your hopes and dreams for the future, the ways you would like to contribute to our society—that will enable you to appreciate and celebrate all aspects of your uniqueness. Developing and enjoying all of these aspects of yourself will combine to give you a capacity for joy and love that will enrich your life immeasurably—whatever your sexual orientation may be!

9

I'm Totally Stressed Out!

I don't have a life basically. Between studying hard to make good grades (so I can get into a good college), doing extracurricular and community service activities (that will look good on a college application), working to (you guessed it!) save money for college plus doing chores my parents expect me to do at home, I have no time for myself or to spend with friends. I don't have any *fun and I wonder, even if I get into a good college, if it will be worth it. I'm so tired all the time and I have constant headaches and worry about keeping my GPA up. Is college worth all this??*

—S.A.

I have awful stomachaches and (this is embarrassing, but true) diarrhea all the time. Sometimes it's worse before an exam or before I have to give an oral report. What's wrong with me?

—Jason L.

I'm upset about everything: starting high school (after going to a small private school through eighth grade), feeling fat (I've put on about twenty pounds in the last year. My parents say it's just normal development, but to me it feels like fat!*) and people expecting more of me now. I just feel like totally overwhelmed and like it's all too much for me. What's wrong with me? I see other people handling things like this just fine.*

—Kelsey D.

What do I owe my parents? I'm having a problem being my own person and it's really upsetting me. I think my dad needs to have me fulfill his dream of being a doctor. He didn't get into medical school and now he wants me to achieve what he couldn't. I'm pretty sure that's not what I want. I'm a good student, but my lowest grades are in science and math. I'm most interested in photography and filmmaking. I'm good at creative things, and even if I didn't make a ton of money doing these, I'd be happy. How can I let my dad know that I need to be my own person in a way he can understand?

—David H.

What these teens are expressing is stress—a feeling of being overwhelmed by life changes, responsibilities, expectations and having too much to do in too little time—and, perhaps, too little fun.

Stress looms large in the lives of young people today. In a recent survey, stress and nervousness emerged as the number one emotional problem voiced by those in the fourteen-to-twenty-one-year-old age group.

Another survey, conducted by University of Michigan

researchers, looked at stress levels of high school juniors in the United States, Japan and Taiwan. The results? American students feel a higher level of stress than their Asian counterparts! This may come as a surprise to those who envision Japanese and Taiwanese students attending classes for long hours six days a week, working with tutors during their "free time" and living with incredible pressure to do well in school. Why are American teens feeling more stress? The answer, researchers contend, lies in the scope of responsibilities and expectations U.S. teens live with. While their Asian counterparts feel pressured to do well in school, American teens feel they need to do well not only in school, but also in sports, friendships/popularity and in after-school jobs. And while school was the number one cause of stress for students in all three countries, high-achieving American students felt the most stress, while high achievers in the other countries felt no more stress than their lower-achieving peers.

You may be feeling stress for a number of different reasons:

- You may be facing a number of changes. Especially in combination, some changes teens normally face can feel stressful. Starting junior high or high school just as puberty hits with a vengeance can be very stressful, as everything from your body to your environment is changing at once. If you're a girl, reaching puberty—starting your period, growing taller, developing breasts and generally assuming an adult woman's shape—when you're in fourth or fifth grade is stressful because you look so different from your peers. (Studies show that early developing boys are seen in a positive way, but many female early bloomers may simply feel fat and uneasy with their own bodies.)

Also, the more adult you *look,* the more people—from teachers to parents to total strangers—expect of you—and that can feel stressful.

Another change is a social one: your friends and peers are more important than ever to you, and at the same time, you're becoming more interested in dating and/or sexual activities. This can cause stress—as you seek to balance your attention and time between boyfriend/girlfriend and your other friends. It can also cause stress if you're feeling different in some way that separates you from your peers—if you're gay or lesbian or if you just don't seem to fit into the dating scene and wonder if anyone will ever love you or find you attractive.

- School can seem newly overwhelming as expectations rise. If you're an excellent student, you may be feeling pressure from parents, teachers, school counselors *and* yourself to make perfect grades, score well on SATs or ACTs, be a student leader and earn as much money as possible to prepare for college. It may feel like running as fast as you can on a treadmill that seems to accelerate constantly. If you're a so-so student, you may be feeling and getting a lot of pressure to pull yourself together and improve your grades so that college, trade school or a spot in the newly

competitive military service will be an option—
and that can be stressful, too. And if you're a student who struggles—perhaps as the result of a
learning disability—you may experience considerable stress as you try your best (sometimes without getting credit for trying so hard), as you
contend with the sneers and jeers of higher
achieving classmates, and maybe even some teachers, and as you wonder if it will always be this
way—trying so hard and never really catching up.

• Your parents may expect much more of you now.
They may expect you to handle many more responsibilities at home and begin to focus more
and more on your future—what they would like
to see you achieve, what they think you should
do with your life. Their expectations can feel
stressful to you, especially if these clash with your
own hopes and dreams for the future.

• You may be putting a lot of pressure on yourself.
You may be a perfectionist—and drive yourself
crazy with your own standards and expectations.
You may put stress on yourself through procrastination—which can make even a simple school
assignment a major ordeal. You may be so anxious
to be accepted by peers that you find it difficult
to say no to your friends, even when a request is
really inconvenient. So you may find yourself doing things, going places or being with people
you'd prefer not to do, go or be with, or taking
on responsibilities you don't want to just because
you don't want to risk disappointing a friend. If
your schedule is crammed with all those "musts,"

you may have little time to do what *you* really want to do—and that can feel stressful.

- There may be a lack of balance in your life. You may be working too hard and not having enough fun. Or you may be goofing off too much and facing the consequences of not meeting your responsibilities. You may have a group of friends who ask a lot of you—and don't give you back the support that you give them so readily. You may be awesome intellectually, but physically out of shape, or you may be in great physical shape, but totally clueless about social or world issues that are part of everyday life for many people. All of this, in various ways, can be stressful.

- You may feel that you lack control over your own life. If you feel that you're on a runaway train made up of others' expectations, societal "have-to's," scary, life-changing decisions and actions that will determine your future, you're going to feel stress—no doubt about it. This is true whether you have a destination or goal in mind—and it is your own idea—or whether you feel all of this is in conflict with what you want for yourself. What causes the stress is the feeling that, day to day, you seem not to have any control over or say in how you are spending your time.

WHAT TO DO IF YOU'RE FEELING STRESSED OUT

✓ *Listen to your body.* Physical symptoms like headaches, stomachaches, gastrointestinal problems, insomnia, loss of appetite or excessive eating, pounding heartbeat and tension in the neck are quite common when you're feeling stressed out. Because these can also be symptoms of medical disorders, it's always a good idea to get a checkup with your physician as a first step toward healing your stress. If you're found basically healthy, despite your symptoms, you'll know that the time has come to take action to manage your stress. Physical symptoms due to stress are an important warning signal that you need to make positive changes in your life.

✓ *Identify your own personal sources of stress.* Before you can begin to calm your body and your mind, you need to know why you're feeling stressed out. Which areas of your life are most stressful? Are there people in your life who cause you to feel stressed out? Ideally, given your own interests now and dreams for the future, how would you choose to spend your time? How far is that from your life as you're experiencing it right now?

It's important to understand that we all have stress in our lives to a certain extent. We all have to do things we don't want to do—and even some of the things we *do* want to do can feel stressful at times. Very few of us ever get to the ideal version of how we'd like to spend our days. However, the closer you can come to the ideal, the greater sense of power you feel to make a difference in your own life, the less discomfort you will feel.

✓ *Realize that you're in control—and how you act and react to the stress in your life can make a major difference.* Taking responsibility for your own feelings and reactions gives you the power to make a difference. If you think that situations involving talking with people you don't know well make you nervous, you may begin positive change toward stress reduction if you can think "I get nervous when I have to talk with people I don't know well." That way, you have the option of doing something within yourself to make this experience less stressful—from pretending that these are old friends, acting as if you aren't shy in such situations or admitting that you're nervous (if that is appropriate) and finding that the other person or people may share your feelings. That can work much better than thinking "Strangers make me nervous" and feeling stressed out and powerless every time you're in such a situation.

It may also help to know that your own perspective can change what might look like a stressful situation into a positive one.

For example, British ice dancers Jayne Torvill and Christopher Dean have with their spectacular routines won two Olympic medals—a gold and a bronze—and the hearts of skating fans all over the world. A recent television special about this famous duo showed another side of their success. During a grueling practice session just before the last Olympics, Dean, who may be as noted for his fiery perfectionism as he is for his skating talent, criticized, nagged and generally ragged on Torvill (as the camera continued to roll) until she cried. It looked like an incredibly stressful—even intolerable—situation until Torvill explained that their combination of talent and very different temperaments is a positive thing: "I'm placid and need to have someone to get me fired up—and Christopher does that!"

You may have a similar situation in your own life—e.g., a teacher who is very tough on you. One choice might be to feel personally persecuted and stressed out. Another choice might be to tell yourself that the teacher cares enough to push you a bit, has enough faith in you to know you can do better. And that may transform what seems hurtful and stressful into a more positive situation in your own mind. Seeing in a new way what feels stressful can make a major difference.

✓ *Make positive changes in your sources of stress.* No matter how powerless you may *feel* in a situation, you always have the power to make a change in the situation itself or in your reaction to it—and thus lower your stress level.

℞ *If you're stressing out over college:* It makes sense to do the best you can in your academic classes, to pursue extracurricular activities *you* enjoy and to do careful research on colleges to determine what might be best for you. Don't just assume that the best will be Harvard or Stanford or some other highly selective school. You need to spend time looking beyond the prestige factor to what *you* really want your college experience to be like. You may find that you prefer a small school or one that is not an academic pressure cooker, or you may prefer the unique vitality of a larger campus or of a highly selective, demanding academic environment. When you start thinking about colleges in terms of *your* needs and not just prestige, the whole experience may begin to seem more accessible and less stressful.

Remember that your life will be happier and, not so incidentally, your college application stronger if you live fully in today, pursuing activities because you enjoy or find value in them, not simply because you think a certain extracurricular activity will look good on an application. In fact, college admissions officials can take one look at your application and tell which things you did for love and which you did to look good in their eyes—and what you did for love always makes the greatest impact.

Remember, too, that colleges—even highly selective ones—are looking for students who are well-rounded *people,* not driven robots who study twenty-three hours a day. For example, admissions interviewers at Northwestern University, a highly selective school near Chicago, are asked to look for a sense of humor in the applicants they see, an ability to relate well and empathize with others and an ability to both work hard *and* have fun. Admissions interviewers there are not likely to ask about GPAs or test scores (those are all on the application), but may well ask "What do you do for fun?" This underscores the belief at many top schools that the healthiest, most likely to succeed students are those with a balance of work and fun in their lives—and a sense of humor that keeps it all in perspective.

So making time for fun can be a crucial element of your healthy development as a person *and* your preparation for college!

℞ *If you suffer from exam jitters:* Tell yourself that whatever happens on this exam, life will go on. That even applies to the SAT or ACT. (Remember that on those exams, you can take them over for higher scores, and many colleges weight GPA and class rank over test scores.) Don't fall into the stressful trap of telling yourself that your whole future hinges on this one test. Tell yourself instead, "No matter what happens with this test, I will be fine." You may be disappointed for a time . . . but you will be fine. Many people with less than wonderful SAT scores have gone to excellent colleges and done well in life. In addition to keeping this sanity-saving perspective, be sure to listen to or read all the instructions on the test and to read over the test before you begin, if that is possible. This will give you time to calm down, follow instructions and pace yourself in the exam. If you find your confidence at an all-time low, answer the easy questions first as a way to build your confidence on the spot (and give yourself more time to think about the more challenging questions!). If you feel yourself starting to tense up, stop for a moment. Close your eyes and breathe deeply. Tell your shoulders, your stomach and your neck muscles (and any other area that may be tense) to relax. Take another deep breath and go on with the test. Keep reminding yourself that no matter what happens with this test, you will be fine and have many other opportunities to succeed in your life.

℞ *You have teacher trouble—big-time:* Think about

why this is happening. Despite the fact that you're feeling stress about this, ask yourself "Whose problem is this?"

If the problem rests with you—you're not doing your assignments, are cutting up in class or otherwise aggravating your teacher—stop and think about why you're doing this. If you dislike the teacher or are bored with the class, think about more positive ways you can deal with the situation. You might choose to see this as a good preparation for the working world, when you won't always be doing work that fascinates you (even the most rewarding career has its tedious tasks) and may well have to work with or for people you wouldn't spend five minutes with otherwise. You might choose to see how you can make a difference: if the teacher is boring or cranky, try thinking of him or her in a new way that highlights any possible strength—like patience or a dry sense of humor. If you can focus on good aspects of the teacher (if any) it can make those minutes (hours!) in the classroom less painful.

You can also make a difference if a subject bores you. Try talking with someone who loves the subject and let some of his or her enthusiasm rub off on you. Do some extra reading or exploring on your own to discover why in the world someone would find this interesting—and you may find your own attitude changing a little. This change, once again, may make sitting through this class less stressful.

Keep in mind that it is less stressful to expand

your own academic horizons and try to put a positive spin on the situation than to make your dislike for the teacher or the subject obvious and deal with the negative consequences.

If you have a teacher who simply lives to give students a hard time, you have a number of choices. You can stay out of this teacher's way as much as possible. You can risk talking with the teacher about how his or her criticism, ridicule or whatever affects you. Or you can seek help and affirmation from others, and accept your difficulty with this teacher as his or her problem—*if* you have done everything possible to improve the situation without success. If it is becoming your problem because the teacher is grading you unfairly, try talking first with your teacher—in the spirit of "I really want to do well. How can I improve in this class?" or "I don't understand why I am getting these grades. Could you give me some suggestions about how I can do better?" It's important to keep your tone respectful—even if you can't stand the teacher and feel he or she is totally unfair. Keeping your own behavior beyond reproach is essential.

If the teacher is abusive, sexist, racist or otherwise averse to being helpful in any way, and you have tried in a respectful manner to change this without success, you may talk with your school counselor or your principal or vice principal to make him or her aware of this and to see what options you might have.

Remembering that you have to put up with this teacher or class for only a semester or a year (as endless as that might seem at the moment) may also help to keep things in perspective—as you mark those days off on your calendar.

℞ *If you're doing the best you can and it still isn't good enough:* If you can honestly say that you are trying your hardest to do as well as you can in school or in learning a new skill or in doing household chores, and your parents are still unhappy with you, you need to talk with each other about what is possible. Something may feel impossible to you: you have such math anxiety that you can't imagine doing well in math, or you're feeling overwhelmed by learning new household tasks and need time before you can do these as well as your parents would like. It may help if you tell your parents about your math anxiety or your difficulty with the new tasks, so that they can help you. It may be that what feels like an incredible burden to you in terms of household responsibilities is just new—or very necessary. That can be especially true if your parent or parents are working several jobs just to make ends meet in a highly uncertain economy. This may simply be a stressful time for your family—and your contribution is very much needed. If you feel truly needed and, to some extent, appreciated, the stress of those extra responsibilities may diminish a bit.

If your parents continue to insist that you should be a straight A student, even though your best efforts elicit C's and an occasional B, it can feel stressful and discouraging.

The first way to deal with these expectations is

to realize that they may be coming from a variety of feelings your parents have. Loving you and wanting the best for you may be blinding them to some of your very real limitations and the reality of what might actually be best for *you*. Your parents may also be living with regrets about their own lives—maybe not having worked hard enough in school or made the most of their own life opportunities—and so they want to make sure that doesn't happen to you. They may even dream of you fulfilling some of their own goals and ambitions. Keep in mind that if your parents aren't happy with themselves, they will find it difficult to be happy with anyone else, including you. It can help to understand that their criticisms, perfectionism and impossible standards are likely to be due more to their dissatisfaction with their own lives or themselves than to a lack of love or lack of valuing you. Remember, too, that your value as a person is not linked to your grades or other achievements. You are a worthwhile person with or without any of these things.

If you are getting punished for not making grades you find impossible to achieve, enlist the help of a teacher or teachers, your school counselor, a caring relative or a clergyperson to talk with your parents. He or she may be able to help your parents to encourage you in more realistic and constructive ways. This person or persons might also be able to help you to feel good about yourself despite your parents' unrealistic expectations.

℞ *If your parents seem determined to plan your whole life for you, and you're wondering if you totally owe them your life:* We owe our parents respect and a listening ear. You can respect their desire for you to do well. You can listen to their dreams, ideas and goals for you. But, ultimately, you owe it to yourself to choose what's right for you and to do the best you can—for you.

If, for example, your parents are urging you to be a doctor or a lawyer and that isn't what you want at all, it still makes sense to do as well as you can in school (which leaves *all* your options open) while dreaming your own dreams. In the long run, when it comes to choosing a career and following it, you may need to risk disappointing your parents by going your own way. However, most parents really want their kids to be happy, and if your parents see that you're happy in pursuing your own dreams, they're likely to come around and be happy for you.

But it's wise to leave yourself room for new dreams and goals—some of which, to your great surprise, might even coincide with what your parents wanted for you.

I remember (this is Kathy speaking) how our father had our futures neatly planned by the time my brother and I were teenagers: I was to be a writer and my brother was to be a doctor. We both said "No way!" Because my father's sister, my beloved Aunt Molly, is a professional writer, I've always known that writing is much more hard work than glamour, and as a teenager, I wanted no part of it. My brother thought being a doctor would be totally gross. Some years went by. My thinking changed during college when I realized that writing was what I did best—and I decided to pursue it as a career in my own way and for my own reasons. (My father wanted me to write fiction, but nonfiction suits me better . . . so that's what I write.)

My brother, in the meantime, started thinking about medical school when he was a fighter pilot in Vietnam. Coming out of the destruction of war, he yearned to be a healer, helping to put back together bodies and lives. So he began medical school in his late twenties and is today a very successful physician at a large medical center. Both of us were chagrined to discover that our father might have been right about our perfect careers all along—but we both feel that our ultimate choices were very much our own and were not made simply to please our father, who, by the way, had the good grace *never* to say "I told you so!"

So it can make sense to keep your parents' dreams for you in a corner of your mind, giving yourself time to see if they may (or may not) be a good fit with your special talents, while also taking time to think about what *you* want out of life.

℞ *Take a close look at your friendship patterns.* Are you giving a lot to your friends in terms of support, a listening ear, positive encouragement and the like but getting little, if any, of the same in return? Do you feel that you can say no to a friend without jeopardizing the friendship—or do you feel you need to give in to what he or she wants all the time in order to keep this friend? All of these patterns of bending to another's needs and wishes while ignoring your own can be incredibly stressful over time. If these patterns pretty much describe your friendships, you need to take action! It is ultimately up to you to break these patterns.

Ask your friends for the support you need. (Friends may have good intentions, but they aren't mind readers.) Try saying no when you need to and see what happens. Some friends may say "Oh, OK" and go on being your friends. Others may turn away from you when you show them that you have a mind and a life of your own. Guess which are the friends worth having?

℞ *If a friend diminishes who you are and what you need as a person, let that friendship go.* A lot of stress will go with it—even though it can hurt to lose a friend. It can be a relief to silence a negative voice, to make a new friend or friends who value you as you are and to have the kind of relationship with your friends that allows you to be yourselves, to voice both positive and negative feelings and to disagree without undermining your basic trust and respect for each other. Those kinds of friendships help you to feel safe in the world, secure with your own uniqueness and cut down on, rather than add to, the stresses of daily living.

℞ *For your own inner demons:* Quite often, the very worst stress we can feel is the stress we put on ourselves via perfectionism, procrastination and anxiety about everything. These particular demons all seem to be related: if you feel anxiety about doing well in a class and think that any effort with less than perfect results is a failure, you may find yourself procrastinating because you so fear not being perfect and thus being a failure in your own eyes.

Cory has this problem with his final papers for classes. He always does wonderfully up to the final paper and then, in a fit of anxiety, finds himself unable to complete the paper in time because he expects perfection—and so finds himself in (totally unnecessary) academic trouble because he hasn't been been turning in his papers on time. Cory would be much better off coming to terms with the fact that no one is perfect—and that being less than perfect doesn't make him a failure.

It's vital to separate who you are from what you do. You are not your work or your grades or your social life. You are much more than you do or achieve. The fact that you exist, in all your uniqueness, is the most special thing about you. When you value who you are as a person, you won't feel immobilized with fear about turning in a paper for a final grade, taking an exam or taking a risk to achieve a goal. When you value yourself, you can say, "I'm going to do my best and that is *all* I can do. If it is less than perfect, it isn't the end of the world." That can free you to *do* your best—and to feel less stressed in the process. I remember (Kathy here again) one evening when I was a teen sitting home in a total snit about a term paper, upcoming exams and the fact that the boy I loved beyond all reason hardly knew I was alive—when the phone rang. It was Mac, an eighty-eight-year-old family friend, who asked how I was doing and who listened kindly as I poured out my troubles. Then, he asked me again, "But how are *you*?"

Thinking for a moment—past all the hassles and worries—to my essence, I replied, with some surprise, "Me? Oh, I guess *I'm* fine!" With his gentle and loving question, Mac had taught me an important lesson: that I was not my work, my grades or my less than exciting social life, but much, much more. I felt immediately relieved and, to my amazement, much better able to concentrate on my studying after that.

℞ *For Impossible Schedules:* When you're going to school, working and otherwise trying to have a life, it can feel stressful just getting through a day or dealing with the unexpected that is threatening to mess up your whole finely tuned schedule.

In order to make an impossible schedule more compatible with your life, cut out nonessentials. This means extra projects, jobs, social activities, and so on that you don't *have* to pursue and don't particularly enjoy. Time spent putting off what *needs* to be done will add stress to your life— when just getting an assignment out of the way so that you can play a little can feel much more satisfying. You also need to limit nonessential "shoulds." There is no life rule that says you have to spend whole evenings on the phone with friends in order to be a good friend. Limit your telephone time if it is longer than you would like and eating up chunks of time you'd rather use to relax or pursue a fun hobby. Taking action to rescue yourself from an impossible schedule means taking a long, hard look at your priorities, at what is important to you, what you must do and what you can let go—and making a new, more flexible schedule for yourself that has room for life's little emergencies and surprises and some breathing space for you.

✓ *Establish balance in your life.* In order to have a truly balanced life, we all need to pay attention to four areas/ aspects of our lives:

Physical: This means listening to and taking good care of our bodies with regular exercise and healthy, nutritious meals and snacks.

Mental: This doesn't simply mean doing the best you can in school, but also keeping up to date and in touch with the world around you, continuing to grow in your understanding of this world and of yourself. Paying attention to your mental development can mean making a habit of thinking about what is important to you, what you want out of life and what you would like to contribute with your own unique talents and gifts.

Emotional: This means not only being in touch with your own feelings, but also forming warm connections with others, giving and receiving love, affection and emotional support.

Spiritual: This may mean practicing the faith of your choice in your local church or synagogue or temple—or it may not. Paying attention to your spiritual side is not confined to practicing an organized religion, but may be as private as realizing your connection to nature and to the universe and finding peace and serenity in this connection.

✓ *Make time for fun.* This is essential in even the most crowded schedule. Take time to do something you really enjoy—writing a letter to a friend or roller-blading or playing with your dog or cat. Think about what fun means to you. Maybe it's a walk by yourself or with a friend through a beautiful forest preserve or park. Maybe it's watching or listening to comedy routines that always crack you up no matter how many times you hear them. Maybe it's being around a friend you especially enjoy and laughing a lot together. Maybe it's doing something silly and spontaneous—like going with a friend for ice cream when it's 10 degrees with snow flurries blowing around you. It can mean trying something you've always wanted to try—like cross-country skiing or cruising the Internet or Karaoke singing. Whatever feels fun for you, make time in your life to do it! Time spent having fun is time well spent. It will replenish your spirit and give you extra strength to withstand the pressures of your life.

✓ *Let others help you.* Support systems are *very* important in all our lives. That's why you need to have friends who will give as well as take, who will be there for you as readily as you are for them. Supportive family relationships are also vital. Some recent studies have shown that teens who have good relationships and communication with their parents can deal with stress most effectively. Other family relationships can be important, too. Maybe you have a brother or sister, a special cousin, an aunt or uncle or a loving grandparent who helps you to laugh, to understand and to weather rough times.

✓ *Keep a journal.* This doesn't have to be a literary masterpiece. It can simply be a for-your-eyes-only way to discover what you're feeling, what feels uncomfortable for you and what action you can take to decrease stress and discomfort in your life or to put a positive spin on it and use it to your advantage. A journal, most of all, can be an exercise in self-awareness.

✓ *Use your imagination to relax.* There may be times when you think wistfully about the peaceful moments in your life. Maybe you were on a camping trip, sitting by yourself in a pine forest, listening to the wind whispering in the treetops and smelling the wonderful scents of the forest. Maybe you were sitting on a beach on an absolutely perfect day, watching the sunlight sparkle on the water and feeling very much at peace. Maybe it was an evening you were in your room listening to your favorite CD and realizing, at that moment, how happy you felt. Maybe it was a moment when you felt warmed and comforted by a loved one's embrace that seemed to shut out the stress and pain you had been feeling.

You can go back to these special moments any time you want via your imagination. You may be in the middle of a tough exam and too anxious to think. Taking a moment to return to that pine forest or that sunny beach or to another place you've found peace may help you to overcome the stress of the moment and concentrate anew on your exam. And if you're feeling stressed out because someone is giving you a hard time, traveling back in time for a moment to that warm embrace and the memory of the encouraging words that may have gone with it can give you the strength to face your current crisis with more confidence and less stress.

✓ *Give yourself the gift of quiet time.* Even if it's only ten or fifteen minutes out of a busy day to meditate, to think or simply to *be,* this quiet time can help a lot in combating stress. This may mean getting up fifteen to twenty minutes earlier than usual (or lying in your bed, fully awake and aware) or taking a long, warm bath at night to get the privacy and space you need. It may mean taking a solitary walk to a place where you feel comfortable and safe, and can sit for a while, thinking your own thoughts, with no immediate sense of urgency.

These quiet moments of reflection are a wonderful gift you can give yourself in order to find the strength, resourcefulness and imagination to face and to contend with all the preventable *and* inevitable stresses of your life!

....

10

I Have an Alcoholic Parent

Beth looks exhausted and very much alone as she struggles to describe her family's private torment.

"My dad drinks—a lot!" she says. "He gets drunk every night and lately has had trouble getting up in the morning to go to work. Sometimes he doesn't get to work until noon, and we're all scared he's going to lose his job. He says he's not an alcoholic, but I think he is because he won't stop drinking even though we've all begged him. I've even hidden his liquor bottles, but nothing works."

A tear slides down her cheek and she wipes it away quickly. "Last night scared me," she continues. "My dad was drunk and yelling at my mom, brother and me, telling us how worthless we are. Finally, I couldn't take it. I grabbed his rum bottle and smashed it in the sink and called him an alcoholic. For a moment, he looked like he was going to kill me. He was so mad, he looked crazy. I was really afraid. And sometimes I don't think I can stand feeling so bad and so afraid anymore. My mom says this is a family matter and we shouldn't talk about it outside the family. But it keeps getting worse and no one in the family really knows what to do."

Beth enraged her father by saying out loud the family secret: her father is afflicted with a disease called alcoholism.

Some people are surprised when they hear alcoholism called a "disease." Many people think it is simply a moral problem or a lack of willpower. But alcoholism is a physical and emotional addiction to alcohol and is recognized as a disease by the American Medical Association. Seeing it as a disease makes it a little more understandable. Just as bulimics binge on food or heroin addicts will do anything for the next fix, the alcoholic is powerless over his or her drinking. It ceases, at some point, to be a conscious act, as the alcoholic loses control over the drinking. Alcoholism is a cruel disease that ravages not only the life and health of the alcoholic, but also the feelings and lives of his or her family.

Even though Beth feels very much alone, she has a lot of company. Thousands of families and teens within these families are affected by alcoholism. And everyone feels very much alone.

The isolation is one of the major aspects of growing up in an alcoholic family. "Don't tell! Don't trust! Keep the secret!" is the unwritten law of the alcoholic family. So members are silenced both by this unspoken rule and by shame.

"I used to live in fear that my mother would be drunk and cause a scene in front of my friends, so I never used to invite friends over—which everyone thought was weird, but I was too embarrassed to tell them," says Zack, now an eighteen-year-old college freshman. "I just never knew what to expect when I'd get home from school. Sometimes, she'd be just fine. Sometimes, she'd be passed out on the couch. And sometimes, she'd be drunk and ranting about how awful everyone was. I was always scared my friends would find out about her. I was just so ashamed—and felt really bad about feeling ashamed of my mom, who is really a good person when she's sober. And, of course, when she's sober, she says that she can stop drinking anytime and makes all kinds of promises that she'll never have another drink. Living with an alcoholic parent is like living with constant fear and shame and disappointment."

Denial of alcoholism is another symptom of the disease. The person who drinks may, like Zack's mother, claim to be able to stop any time. Or he or she may make excuses like these:

"I only drink beer and just to relax. Nothing wrong with that."

"Give me a break. You'd drink, too, if you were raising two teenagers!"

"Look, I'm not a skid row bum. I have a good job and I work hard. If I want to have a few drinks, I'll have a few drinks."

The family may slip into this denial as well, telling themselves that the alcoholic can stop drinking anytime, especially if the family helps. And guilt may abound as kids wonder if they asked less of the parent or kept their rooms cleaner or made better grades, worried the parent less, if the drinking would stop. The answer, of course, is no.

An alcoholic may drink wine or beer or hard liquor. He or she is more likely than not to hold a job and have a family. What matters is not *what* the alcoholic drinks or *why* the alcoholic says he or she drinks, but the fact that the drinking is out of control and is interfering with his or her life and that of the family.

To be part of an alcoholic family is to feel hopeless and helpless—for alcoholism is a progressive disease that only gets worse until the alcoholic can find his or her own reasons to get sober. Begging and pleading won't help. Hiding or smashing liquor bottles won't help. Showering him or her with love won't help. One of the most painful realities of having an alcoholic parent is realizing that you are powerless to keep your parent from drinking.

There may be times when your parent may accuse you of causing the drinking, either directly (a comment like "If you had two teenagers, you'd drink, too!") or indirectly (with general comments about the difficulty of being a parent).

"It kills me inside when my dad goes on about how his life is just hell since he had kids and how happy he and mom were before they were parents," says Cara, sixteen. "He's always going on to Mom like 'Remember how happy we were BC?' BC, of course, means 'Before Cara.' It makes me feel terrible and like I'm somehow responsible for his unhappiness and his drinking."

But Cara, of course, is not to blame. She is not responsible for her father's drinking, nor can she control it.

That can feel pretty hopeless until you realize that, as bad as your home situation may be, you *do* have the power to change your own life.

WHAT TO DO IF YOU HAVE AN ALCOHOLIC PARENT

✓ *Realize that it's not your fault—and the only person you can be responsible for is yourself.* You didn't cause your parent's alcoholism and you can't control or cure it. But you *can* take action to improve your own life, as difficult as living with an alcoholic parent can be.

✓ *Join Alateen.* This is a group for teenagers with alcoholic parents and is affiliated with Alcoholics Anonymous. There are chapters of this group at thousands of locations across the country. You can get in touch with the one closest to you by looking in the white pages of your phone book for Alateen or Alcoholics Anonymous. You can join Alateen whether or not your parent is a member of AA. Even if you're not typically a joiner, this can be a very positive move. Some of the most painful aspects of living in an alcoholic family, as we have seen, are the secretiveness, the denial, the lack of support as all attention is focused on the alcoholic, and the isolating shame that keeps you from confiding in your friends. At Alateen, you will meet people with whom you can talk freely, who will keep everything said in the group confidential and who will understand completely what you have to say, because they've all been there, too. Alateen will help you to realize, in new ways, your separateness from your alcoholic parent and your responsibility for yourself. In such a group, you can learn to act in ways that *don't* enable your parent's alcoholic behavior, and at the same time, share your feelings with people your own age. Knowing that you are not alone and that you *can* cope with this very difficult situation can be a great comfort.

✓ *Let go of your desire to change your parent, and focus on yourself.* This isn't selfish. It's necessary. You don't have the power to change your parent and you don't help your alcoholic parent with constant pleas to get sober. Remember that this is a growing time for you. This is a time when you need to pay attention to your own physical and mental health, to your own intellectual and emotional development. Granted, it can sometimes feel silly to try to have a normal life—doing homework, seeing friends, spending quiet time thinking about who you are becoming and your future goals—when you're living in a home made chaotic by an alcoholic parent. But, for your own sake, you need to seek out the support and the space you need to keep your own life as normal as possible.

✓ *Stop rescuing and start loving your alcoholic parent in a new way.* It's easy—out of love and desperation—to fall into rescuing behavior: making excuses for your alcoholic parent, calling in to work to say he or she has the flu, picking him or her off the floor, neglecting your own needs (e.g., to do homework, to spend time with friends) to keep your parent company because he or she demands it or because you feel that if you just love your parent enough, he or she will stop drinking. The hard bottom line about alcoholism is this: your parent will not stop drinking until things get very bad, very uncomfortable, until he or she hits "rock bottom" as AA calls it. "Rock Bottom" doesn't necessarily mean that he will lose a job and the family will be out on the street before the alcoholic will be motivated to seek treatment. But it means that when you cover up or somehow lessen the discomfort of the consequences of your parent's drinking, you help your parent to postpone that time when he or she finds drinking too uncomfortable to continue and is motivated to get help. Wanting to help is a common and understandable reaction. But the motivation to change has to come from within your parent and from the pain of feeling the consequences of his or her alcoholism.

Loving your parent in a new way may mean showing love and attention when he or she is sober. It can mean acting as if your parent were not an alcoholic during moments of sobriety—asking his or her opinions or advice, sharing good things as well as concerns in your life. In essence, it means trying to have as normal a parent-teen relationship as possible when your parent is sober enough to do so. It can be tempting, when you're feeling such disappointment over the ugly words said under the influence of alcohol and all the promises broken, to want to shut your alcoholic parent out of your life. Keep in mind that your parent has a disease. If, for example, your parent had epilepsy instead of alcoholism, you might be frightened by the seizures and feel helpless to prevent or control them. But you would feel love and compassion for your parent nonetheless and would try hard to have a normal, loving relationship with him or her during the times between seizures. Try thinking about your parent's alcoholism in the same way. It's normal to feel upset, helpless and depressed when the symptoms of your parent's disease are present. But if you can make the most of the times in between, this love can go a long way toward making your relationship with your parent as rewarding as possible.

✓ *Protect yourself—even if it means breaking the family code of silence.* If your alcoholic parent is endangering your life by insisting that you ride in the car he or she insists on driving while drunk, or falling asleep with lit cigarettes, you need to seek help and to protect yourself. If your alcoholic parent is abusing you physically or sexually, you need to break the silence and get help. If your other parent cannot help you (often the nonalcoholic spouse is so preoccupied with the alcoholic that he or she may be unable to hear your distress), talk with another adult: a family member, a teacher or counselor or clergyperson. It can be scary to risk revealing the family secret, but there are times when that is the only way you and your family can get the help you so desperately need.

✓ *If your alcoholic parent is in treatment or is sober, realize that this is a process and take things one day at a time.* Perhaps you've spent a lot of time dreaming about what life would be like if only your alcoholic parent could get treatment and stop drinking. Now your parent has, but life still doesn't feel normal. Your parent seems to spend as much time at AA meetings as he or she used to spend at bars. Your parent is cranky and irritable, ragging on you about the smallest thing. And you may find yourself super-vigilant about any slipups he or she may have and scared to death that the drinking will start all over again. While life in recovery may be better, it's not likely to be idyllic. Recovery from alcoholism takes time.

For a while, your parent may well need to spend a lot of time at AA and may be cranky (not only is your parent overcoming a physical addiction, but also he or she is having to face the stresses of daily life without the soothing effect of alcohol). The best way to deal with this time is to tell yourself that, along with the recovering alcoholic, you will take life "one day at a time." Each day that the alcoholic manages not to drink is a victory and a step toward full recovery.

Keep in mind, too, that many people believe that alcoholism is always with the afflicted person, who may make the daily decision to stay sober, but who may never be able to drink like a normal person and who may always need some support from AA or another recovery group to stay sober. So life may not ever be the same as it was before your parent became an alcoholic . . . but it can get better, one day at a time.

✓ *Realize that your life will be affected by your parent's alcoholism for years to come—in positive and negative ways.* Feelings and memories may linger for a lifetime, and you may make certain life choices because of these.

Kevin still remembers the terrible stomach pains he felt when walking home from school on his father's paydays, praying all the while that his father hadn't spent the money already at the local bar. The memories of his family's pain—the drunken fights, the promises broken and the financial desperation—are never far away. But Kevin made a vow to build a very different life for himself. He chooses not to drink at all. He is a respected and compassionate· high school teacher and counselor with special empathy for teens whose parents are alcoholics.

Jill remembers hating her alcoholic father, "who broke every promise he ever made to my mom and me." For some time after she left home for college, she had trouble trusting *any* man. Recognizing that this was a problem for her, she sought therapy. Good therapy and her own determination to change have brought rich rewards to Jill: a normal, loving family—a husband she trusts implicitly and two healthy children.

How will you choose to live with the present realities and the memories of growing up with an alcoholic parent? You have a lot of choices.

You can choose *not* to follow in your parent's unhappy—even tragic—pattern, by not drinking (or drinking very moderately) and by not getting romantically involved with someone with even the hint of a substance abuse problem. (Don't be too quick to dismiss the latter as absolutely impossible: many people choose to date and marry people who are somehow similar to their families of origin—even if those similarities are destructive, like alcoholism.)

You can choose to suffer for a lifetime for your pain of today or you can use it to grow. In the past decade, there has been increased attention given to the lives and feelings of adult children of alcoholics—called ACAs by the recovery movement. While this increased awareness of the lifetime impact that parental alcoholism can have is a good thing, the dark side of this new awareness is that some people choose to use it as an excuse for all the problems of their lives or for their own failures and shortcomings. So they get stuck in perpetual victimhood, feeling helpless and in pain and angry at and blaming their parents.

Another choice you can make is to acknowledge the fact that you've grown up with a lot of pain and then get on with your life—building a happy, productive life for yourself whether or not your parent *ever* gets sober.

Remember: the only life you can change is your own!

....

11

It Hurts to Be Different

Nobody likes me much at school because I'm not a jock and my personality is kind of shy. Inside, I feel like I'm a good person, but no one cares about that at my school. I can't stand how lonely I feel.

—Greg J.

I'm fat, really fat! I weigh 241 and I'm five-six and people at school treat me like an outcast. They make fun of everything I do and laugh about how fat and ugly I am. There is this one guy who starts barking every time he sees me. I just want to die! I've tried diets, but nothing works. Even my family is totally disgusted with me. I feel like I'm missing out on everything good about being young. Help!

—Mandy Y.

I go to this boring school where I don't fit in. Not at all. Everyone is white except me (I'm black) and some Asian

*students who hang out together and study most of the time.
Mostly, people ignore me or stare at me. And when people
say "Hi" I get the feeling like they feel they have to or they
think they're doing me a favor. One girl said she thought
it must be hard to be the only black person here and asked
me how I felt about it, but that just made me mad. Like
I could explain racism in twenty-five words or less! I told
her she didn't have a clue and would never know what it's
like to be me so it's pointless to explain. A teacher who
overheard said I was being rude. I feel like no one under-
stands or even tries to understand things from my point of
view.*

—Keeshia

*I swear I'm the only person I know who doesn't have a
boyfriend. I'm not especially ugly or especially pretty. I try
to be nice. But I feel left out of everything!*

—B.N.

*My problem is that I'm am average person in this school
where everyone is into being the best. I'm in special ed
because of a learning problem and people call me a "re-
tard." All they talk about is how they're going to Harvard
and stuff. There's nobody for me to talk to and be friends
with.*

—Hayden D.

Being different can hurt—a lot!

It can hurt to look different from most of your peers—
to be overweight or unusually tall or short or have a
physical problem that shows—at a time when everyone
tries to look pretty much the same in order to be con-

sidered "normal." Some of these conditions may change with time, while some won't. But, whatever happens later on, looking and feeling different can dramatically influence how you feel about yourself right now.

It can hurt to feel limited, victimized or isolated by racism. Even if someone at school tries to understand, you may feel that no one who is white could possibly understand how it feels to be African-American, Latino or Asian in a Eurocentric culture. So why bother trying to explain how you feel or to get along, when it's so easy to be misunderstood and so hard to communicate what a difference one's ethnicity can make in the way society views you—and you view society? You may feel a painful combination of sadness, rage and loneliness as you live with your differentness.

It can hurt to feel different because of special medical needs: the diabetes that requires you to eat a balanced diet on a regular schedule, to test your blood sugar and take insulin injections; the epilepsy that postpones or prevents your getting a driver's license; or any other physical challenge that sets you apart in some way from your peers.

It can hurt, too, to feel different for no special reason except you just don't fit in somehow, at school or in your own family, where everyone else is one way and you're quite another.

THREE THINGS TO REMEMBER WHEN YOU'RE FEELING DIFFERENT AND DOWN

1. *Being different does* not *mean being inferior.* There is something special about you. It may

take time to accept yourself and discover all your special qualities, but it's well worth the effort.

2. *Being a member of the* in *group at school is no guarantee of happiness or of a lifetime of achievement.* If you feel out of the charmed inner circle at your school, you have lots of company (even though you may feel very much alone)!

What makes one in? While at some highly competitive schools it may mean excelling academically, typically in group status is gained with athletic ability, looks, cheerleading, nice clothes and/or a winning personality.

Author Ralph Keyes, whose book *Is There Life After High School?* quickly hit best-seller charts several years ago (showing how many of us had less than wonderful high school years!), observed that "Being in has nothing to do with ability. Power is central. This power comes from things that are given to a person—like looks, family status or clothes. These things are bestowed, not earned, and so those who possess them feel little pride in the attainment of this power. Many in group people, amazingly enough, don't feel especially popular. Some fear others like them only for their status and not for themselves."

Also, being popular in high school is not a sign that even better things are on the horizon. Some high school stars peak in their teens and spend the rest of their lives looking back to that time of glory. Others with less stellar high school experiences go on to have very happy and successful lives and careers. Being out of it in high school is not a sign that you're a loser. It may simply mean that your time of greatest happiness is yet to come.

Life usually does improve after high school, not because you are suddenly and magically transformed, but because your environment and what works in this environment change. As you build a career and/or your own family, cuteness, athletics and a great car matter less than imagination, intelligence, compassion, patience and quiet persistence.

"No study I read in researching my book has found any correlation between high status in high school and achievement as an adult," says Ralph Keyes.

So even if your life is less than wonderful now, there *is* hope for the future!

3. *Being* out *of the inner circle gives you more options*. You don't have to hang out with people you don't like or live up to any kind of image. You can simply be yourself and make good friends of your own choosing. And when you're choosing friends, the best, most lasting ones may be those who are kind, who understand how loneliness feels, who value in others many qualities besides the "givens".

WHAT TO DO WHEN FEELING DIFFERENT HURTS

✓ *Ask yourself what—if anything—you're willing to give up in order to fit in.* How would you need to change in order to fit in? Would this change be beneficial to you or would it take something vital away from the unique person you are?

For example, statistics show that, despite the fact that girls tend to do very well in all subjects in elementary school, academic achievement—especially in subjects like math and science—tends to drop among girls in junior high. This is a time when many girls feel pressure to have a boyfriend and may fear that guys won't like someone who excels in traditionally "male" subjects or who outshines them in the classroom. If this sounds like your situation (even a little), you have some choices. The easy way out—with benefits for now and drawbacks for later—is to make having a boyfriend your first priority and let your studies slide. Holding on to the person you are—who may be good in math and have hopes and ambitions for the future—may be a little harder today, but may bring many benefits in the future. Keep in mind that boys tend to be quite insecure in early adolescence and may feel threatened by strong girls. But it won't always be that way. As they grow and mature—in the later years of high school and beyond—they are better able to appreciate smart, independent women. So hanging on to your dreams and being your own person won't mean being dateless forever—and you may even discover a special person soon who appreciates the real you!

The best, most lasting love relationships seem to come into your life when you're busy being yourself and doing things you enjoy.

Sometimes, however, what you need to give up in order to fit in better with peers might be to your advantage.

For example, if you're shy, making yourself reach out a little more—taking risks that are a little scary to you—may bring you new friends and a new outlook on life. You may be capable of doing so much more than you ever imagined!

If you have an attitude that puts others off—say, you're smart and use your intelligence to put others down or, perhaps, you're really angry about being a victim of discrimination and tend to write off people of other ethnicities as impossibly racist and generally uncaring—making some fine adjustments to your outlook and behavior can bring big rewards. This doesn't mean acting dumb or trying to deny your ethnicity. It means giving others a chance: appreciating their insights and intelligence (there are many different kinds of intelligence, after all) and personal qualities or giving them the benefit of the doubt in terms of caring and being open to your life experience and your point of view.

In the same way, if you're besieged with taunts and teasing because you're overweight or because you're not good at sports, ask yourself what you would need to give up and what you might gain as the result of making a change. Your solution/answer may not be simple. You may be using food and weight as a cushion against deeper hurt or as an expression of your pain. Before you even consider changing your eating and exercise habits to shed that extra weight, you might want to think about finding new ways to deal with pain or anger or sadness. When you take care of those needs in a positive way, you'll be better able to take care of yourself in terms of maintaining a healthy body weight. And if you're notoriously awful at sports, think about what it might be like to take some lessons, practice more or look for a sport you might manage better. It's one thing to be absolutely horrible or really fantastic at a sport. It's quite another to be just average, so-so or only semi-bad—most people fall into these categories in most sports. If you find a sport you really enjoy, perhaps you won't mind the fact that you're not especially good at it. If you only try what you think you'll do well, you'll find yourself missing out on a lot of fun, good exercise and some surprising discoveries about your own abilities (including the ability to laugh at yourself).

✓ *If you decide to make changes, make them for your own benefit, not for others.* Deciding to change something that makes you different only because others tease you or nag you, or because you dislike yourself and feel that losing weight or surgically altering a large nose or protruding ears will change who you are, is not the answer to your misery. You need to love and accept yourself just as you are today. You need to believe that you are a good, worthwhile person no matter what you weigh or how you look or what other people say. Then you can choose quite affirmatively to make a positive change for your own health and satisfaction. To be lasting and positive, however, that change has to come from feelings of self-love—wanting to take better care of yourself—instead of self-hate.

✓ *Cultivate your differentness in a positive way.* If, for example, being different has brought you pain, use that pain to develop insight and compassion for others who may be feeling bad, too. (It may be a temptation to lash out in anger at everyone when you're feeling disliked, or to reject others before they have a chance to reject you, but these tactics only make you feel worse.) And if you look around, you'll notice that not everyone who seems happy or well liked is perfect. But these people don't let a difference—be that a difference in size, talents, life experiences or ethnicity—stand between them and others.

For example, Lisa is a seventeen-year-old senior at a Los Angeles area high school that has a large Asian student population, a somewhat smaller white contingent and a sprinking of Latino and African-American students. The groups don't mix well at Lisa's school, and as an Asian-American with a desire to have friends of all colors, Lisa has been frustrated by the racial isolation at her school. "It was terrible because I felt pressure not to be just another clannish Asian student, but, on the other hand, I felt pressure from other Asian students to be loyal to the group, and I felt like I didn't belong anywhere," she says. "What I finally decided was that I couldn't change or have power over another person's behavior, but I could over my own. I decided to try making friends with some people of other races whom I had met and liked at school. I found that I gained a lot of self-respect when I did this, when I listened to my own heart and did what I wanted to do. And I didn't get cut off from my Asian friends. I think, in some way, they respect me more for being different. And maybe sometime soon, some of them will widen their own friendship circles. But I can't force them to do that. I can only do what I think is best for me."

✓ *If you're upset because you have no friends, ask yourself what kind of a friend you are—or could be.* This may mean asking yourself some tough questions if you've been losing a lot of friends lately. For example:

- Do you have a need to be right all the time? Are you judgmental about others' feelings or actions, making it clear that *your* way of thinking is the *only* way? In your efforts to win points and arguments, you may be losing friends.
- Do you neglect your friends—forgetting they exist when you're in love or always waiting for them to call *you* or expecting them to sit for hours listening to your problems but not offering them a patient listening ear when they need to talk?
- Are you loyal to your friends? Do you keep their secrets, defend them against lies or gossip or verbal attacks, comfort them when they're sad and stand by them in crisis times as well as happy times?
- Are you willing to give as well as take? Friendship doesn't mean trading favor for favor, but it does mean caring about each other. Do you use a friend as a sounding board for your own problems, but find yourself unwilling to switch gears when it's *your* turn to listen? Do your friends mean enough to you that you're willing to work out problems together instead of simply dropping a friend at the first sign of trouble?

It's often said—but it's true—that in order to have good friends, you need to *be* a good friend—and that's something you can start doing and being today!

✓ *Take the risk of reaching out.* It may feel scary at first. You might feel incredibly vulnerable or even silly, but deciding to say "Hi" first, acting as if people like you and greeting them in a friendly way, asking questions or starting conversations, can bring rewards as well as rejections.

When he first came to his high school in a small farming community, Le Nguyen, sixteen, was a total outcast. A Vietnamese immigrant in a sea of white faces, he struggled with his English skills and with terrible loneliness as he ate lunch by himself day after day. One day, he made a decision that changed his life: "I decided to run for class president," he says with a wide grin. "I figured that running for office would force me to talk to people and that once they got to know me, they would think I was OK. So whether or not I won the election, I figured I might win some friends!"

In classic hare and tortoise tradition, Le found himself running against the class jock, who assumed he had the election in his pocket. Le, on the other hand, campaigned eagerly, table-hopping in the cafeteria to talk with classmates, getting to know people in and out of class, covering bulletin boards with his campaign materials. His classmates were fascinated and many came to admire his courage. He won decisively—and his life has been full of friends and activities since. He started a peer counseling program at the high school and led his classmates in becoming involved with wide-reaching community services and activities. His journey from outcast to one of the most popular and admired students in his school started with his own decision to change his own life.

✓ *Do something nice for someone else.* In addition to making someone else's life happier or easier for a moment or today, this will help you to feel better about yourself and more confident about reaching out to others in all ways.

What random acts of kindness can you try? You might start by saying hello to someone you usually ignore or apologizing to someone you may have hurt. Or you might do volunteer work in your community or with your church and perhaps meet some new friends in the process. You might rediscover a friendship you've neglected and make a decision this time to give that friend the loyalty he or she deserves. You might give a sincere compliment to someone who is usually ignored or start a conversation with someone who is shy. You might teach someone else a new skill or tutor a classmate who is struggling.

The possibilities are endless and so are the rewards.

✓ *Let others know how you feel.* This can mean sharing your sadness, discomfort, hurt or anger with those who care or can help you make a difference.

For example, if you are the different one in your family or you find that your parents treat you quite differently from a sibling, talk to them in a respectful but honest way, letting them know how this feels to you. This can be a much more positive move than slinking off to sulk and assume that you're unloved. Seek help and reassurance from those you love. It can help to share your tears.

Even with people you don't know as well, it can help to be very much yourself. When I (this is Kathy speaking) first went away to school, I walked into my dorm room, took one look at my roommate (a total stranger) and felt a stab of homesickness so horrendous that I sat down at my desk and pretended to read a newspaper for over an hour before I could get a grip and stop crying. I never said anything to my roommate, Cheryl (who ended up being a dear friend to this day), about how scared and lonely I felt. Many years later, when Cheryl and I happened to take a short vacation together, she asked me about that first day. "When you sat there reading the newspaper for *two hours,* were you crying?" she asked gently. I asked her how she knew. She smiled. "Because you sat there for two hours and never turned a page," she said. "All the time, I was wishing we could talk. I felt lonely, too. I had just finished crying before you walked in. Wouldn't it have been nice if we could have comforted each other that first day?" Yes. It would have been nice to know I wasn't quite so alone. It would have felt a little scary (because I didn't want my roommate to think I was a big baby), but it might well have been a risk worth taking.

If your painful feelings of being different come from others' teasing or thoughtless comments, it might help to let them know that this isn't OK with you. If they're friends or potential friends, they'll make an effort to stop hurting you. If they're bullies or out to get you, you might, quite wisely, keep from letting them know just how much they hurt you. But tell *someone* who can comfort and reassure you—a parent, a relative who cares, a friend or, in a pinch, your diary or even your ever-loyal pet (pets can make great confidantes because they always love you and keep secrets!).

✓ *Don't pass up possible friendships out of fear of being labeled.* If you're feeling lodged in the outer reaches of your school's *out* group, you may fear being further labeled by having friends who are different, too. But some of these may prove to be your most valuable and lasting friendships. "I was totally shocked when Ben, this guy I knew from math class who was one of the few people who talked to me, told me he was gay," says Ryan, seventeen. "I thought that everyone in school would know and that they'd think I was gay, too, if I hung out with him. I kind of avoided him for a few days, but I found that I missed talking to him. I finally decided that Ben was a good friend and that making a friendship worth having was more new important than what people who didn't care about me anyway thought. In the past two years, I've really enjoyed having him for a friend and I've also found that most people at school are pretty cool about differences like being gay. I think it's more of a worry for parents, who are afraid their kids will turn gay or something if they hang out with a gay friend, than for teenagers. Ben and I respect each other's differences. He knows I'm straight—and he likes me anyway!"

✓ *If you're having trouble making friends at school, try making friends outside of school.* You may even meet and rediscover people from school in a more agreeable setting. Try church activities, volunteer work, community theater, community service or other activities you enjoy. You may get to know some people from your school outside their usual cliques. You may meet new friends who share your interests. And you may begin to feel good about yourself by doing something worthwhile, something that you love. These good feelings may carry over into your school experience, boosting your confidence and your ability to make new friends.

✓ *Make a truce with your world—and with yourself.* The pain of being different can make you bitter—or it can make you stronger and wiser.

So you feel that it isn't fair because your difference puts you at a disadvantage or has you firmly and seemingly forever in your school's out group. You're right. Life *isn't* fair a lot of the time. The "isms" like racism, sexism or looksism unfairly hurt and limit the potential of many good, talented and deserving people.

Accepting the fact that this unfairness exists does not mean saying it's OK. It doesn't mean that you accept limits or impose them on yourself. It means that you start by making a difference in your own life, by not letting bitterness and despair kill your spirit. You can use your anger in positive ways—to strengthen your resolve to have a happy, productive life despite its inherent unfairness and to make an effort in your own way, your own style, to try to change patterns of thinking and acting that perpetuate those life-limiting "isms."

Although it may seem impossible, feeling pain now may leave a lasting impression—and make you more compassionate toward others (and yourself) for a lifetime.

It may actually be an advantage (hard to believe but true) *not* to be the most popular, most admired person in your school. Why? Because when you're watching from the sidelines, a little heartbroken, a *lot* insecure, you may realize that friendships do not come easily for you right now—and so decide to work harder on being a good friend and on treasuring the friends you do have. Taking the time to develop your own capacity to give in friendship, accepting your own strengths and your own imperfections as well as those of your friends, realizing that good friendships are worth nurturing and keeping, will bring you some wonderful friends and much personal growth now and in the years to come.

12

Someone I Love Has Died ... and I Don't Think I'll Ever Be Happy Again

"I couldn't believe the sun could shine so bright and the day could be so beautiful and people on the street could be going around as if nothing ever happened on a day when my whole world fell apart," says Kim, seventeen, remembering her mother's death from cancer last year. "I knew she might die, but as sick as she was, I never really believed that she would. When she died, I stood there numb. My heart beat really fast and I was screaming on the inside and shaking on the outside. But for a time, I couldn't say anything. After a little while, I started crying and it felt like I would never stop. My grandparents tried to comfort me and told me they'd take care of Brian and me. But it was the loneliest feeling ... sometimes it still is. And I wonder if I'll ever be happy, really happy, again."

Chris still gets tears in his eyes when he remembers his brother's death in a car crash—caused by a drunk driver—eight months ago. "It didn't have to happen but it did and that makes me furious," he says, looking down at his hands, clenched in his lap. "He was just going over to his girlfriend's house. I had just talked with him. Then he was gone . . . just like that. My parents were just . . . well, you know. I'm scared our family will never be the same. Sometimes they act like I'm not even here and I wonder if they wish I had died instead of Brad. And that hurts—a lot!"

Dan is still reeling from the shock of two deaths: his best friend Sean died of leukemia three months ago, after an intense, painful two-year battle with the disease, and just last week, his beloved golden retriever was hit by a car. He finds himself constantly on the verge of tears. "I'm crying for Sean and for Charlie, my dog, and it feels stupid to feel as bad about my dog as I do my best friend," he says, fiercely wiping a tear away. "But I can't help it. If people at school knew that I cry myself to sleep every night thinking about my dog, they'd think I was crazy!"

There is nothing crazy about grief—even though it can turn your world upside down and make you wonder about your sanity at times. Grief is a natural response to loss. It's a process that involves a lot of different feelings—and no two people experience grief in quite the same way. Some people cry a lot at the funeral; others are still in shock, still numb and disbelieving. Some people feel a lot of anger along with their sadness—anger at the person for dying and leaving them, anger at God for allowing such a terrible thing to happen, anger at themselves for all the words left unsaid or conflicts unresolved, anger at others whose lives are going along as yet untouched by death. Other people don't experience anger, just profound sadness and a feeling that life will never be the same.

Your feelings can differ, too, depending on the person who died and how he or she died.

When a grandparent dies, for example, you may feel that you have lost an incredibly special person in your life, an ally, a dear friend, *or* your grandparent may have been a loving but distant person in your life or someone you've never really known.

When a parent dies, on the other hand, it changes your life profoundly. Not only have you lost a primary person in your life, but also your family will change—in its roles, relationships, circumstances, finances and the like. You have lost a sense of security, a sense that your parents will always be there for you. Even if the parent who dies does not live with you, the final loss of this relationship may be a crushing blow. It can feel as bad when you lose a parent you don't get along with as when you lose a parent you adore, because death brings the loss of hope that anything will ever be different. You can't continue to hope for closeness someday or improved communication. And letting go of that hope is very hard.

When a sibling dies, it also changes your family profoundly. Like Chris, you may feel shut out by your parents' grief even as you grieve for the lost companionship of your sibling. There may be times when, like Chris, you wonder if your parents wish that you had died instead. If you were particularly close to your sibling and/or this death leaves you an only child, the impact of this loss may be even greater.

A friend's death can bring almost unbearable pain—

and what's rough is that because this person wasn't a relative many people will not realize how much this is hurting you. In many instances, you may feel closer to a friend—someone you chose to love—than you are to some of your relatives, and the loss of that friend may cause intense grief. When a friend dies young, it changes you, too. You begin to lose the sense that nothing bad can happen, that you and your friends will be forever young and somehow immortal. The death of a friend shatters that illusion forever—and so, as you grieve for your friend, you may also be grieving at the realization of your own mortality. That isn't crazy. It's a normal and understandable feeling to have.

If a beloved pet dies, the loss can be devastating. Pets are wonderful because they don't judge. They love you no matter what. And they cuddle up with you when you're sad or sullen or scared and even seem to listen if you say your feelings out loud. They ask so little and give so much . . . and when you lose a pet, it can be overwhelming. At the same time, like Dan, you may feel stupid for feeling so sad about a cat or dog or other animal. Even though you *know* this animal was different, special, you keep telling yourself to calm down (before you hear the same thing from others) with "Oh, for heaven's sake! Get a grip! It was just a cat." The fact is, the loss of an animal you love can hurt as much as the loss of a person. It isn't crazy. It isn't stupid. It's a fact.

The circumstances of a person's death can affect you deeply, too.

If a grandparent you don't know well dies in another state and you don't attend the funeral, the death may seem less real and affect you less than if the grandparent had lived nearby.

If a loved one has died after a long and painful illness, you may have had a long time to grieve about his or her fatal illness and feel some measure of relief that your loved one's suffering is over. At the same time, death is always something of a surprise when it happens and is a great loss when it comes to someone you love so much.

When a loved one dies suddenly, shock and disbelief may linger longer than if the death were expected. You may grieve not only the loss of your parent or sibling or friend, but also the fact that you never had a chance to say good-bye or "I love you" one last time.

When someone you love is murdered, or killed because of someone else's carelessness or thoughtlessness (as in drunk driving), anger may play a larger role in your grieving process, as you feel rage at the person who caused your loved one's death. If there is a trial involved, you may find that some of your healing grief gets put on hold by anger until the legal aspects are resolved. Then the tears may come. That doesn't happen with everyone, of course, but it is not uncommon.

As we said, the process of grief is ongoing and different for every individual. However, there are some very common aspects of grief that most people feel at some point.

These include the following:

NUMB DISBELIEF

This is most common when you've just seen or heard that someone you love has died. You feel otherworldly, like a robot or on automatic pilot. You may look out the window and see life going on outside and wonder how that is possible on a day when something so terrible has happened. You may hear yourself saying "My dad died" and be a little startled by how calmly you say it. You may take care of other people around you who are totally falling apart and be amazed or upset that you aren't crying or can't seem to cry. This isn't a sign that you're a terrible, unfeeling person or going out of your mind. This part of the grief and healing process is protective. It keeps you from feeling the full burden of loss all at once. It's much the same when you sprain an ankle or break a bone. You feel that awful, wrenching pain, a sick feeling at the pit of your stomach, and your heart may race. But then, for a time, you feel kind of spacy and numb, before the real, throbbing pain sets in. It can be that way with the grief process, too, as the sharpness of your pain is muted a bit at first to allow you to begin to take it all in, instead of being absolutely overwhelmed.

DENIAL

Now the numbness has worn off and you have moments of feeling the tremendous pain of loss. But it isn't constant. There are still times when you can't quite believe it. There are times when, deep down, you refuse to believe that this person you loved so much is no more. You may pick up the phone, expecting to hear the person's voice. You may catch a glimpse of him or her . . . just a glimpse in a crowd and have a moment of pure joy until you realize that it's not your loved one.

You may absentmindedly set the table for that person, talk to the person as if he or she were still with you, and catch yourself referring to him or her in the present tense. All of that is a normal part of the grieving process, especially at first, as you struggle to comprehend this loss. You may also find yourself experiencing other forms of denial that can stall your grief process—such as refusing to deal with the fact of your loss at all, busying yourself with schoolwork or activities or simply acting as if nothing unusual had happened—because, deep down, you just can't bear the reality of your loss.

Sometimes, too, you may feel you don't have the option to fully grieve your loss at the time it happens. Holly was fourteen when her father, to whom she was very close, died in a work-related accident. Her mother collapsed into a prolonged clinical depression, leaving Holly to handle all household details and the daily care of her younger sister. "I couldn't cry after my dad died," Holly remembers. "I was afraid if I started crying, I'd never stop, and I had to handle everything because my mom couldn't. I married my husband right after high school graduation two years ago and we celebrated our first anniversary with the birth of our son! My father's death hit me suddenly a few months ago as I watched Ray give our son his bottle. I suddenly started crying and saying over and over 'My daddy's dead! My daddy's dead!' Part of what made me feel that then was seeing Ray be such a loving daddy to Tyler. He reminded me suddenly of my dad. But another part of it was that I felt safe and loved and taken care of . . . and so I could finally let down my guard and really feel those really painful feelings and know that someone would be there for me."

ANGER

As we discussed earlier in this chapter, anger can be a part of grief. You may be angry at God, at the person who died, at people who haven't had anything bad happen to them and at yourself for a myriad of reasons.

For example, when Terri's father died of a heart attack at his office, she felt enraged at him for dying without saying good-bye and, at the same time, was furious at herself. "I had a fight with him the night before he died, about something that was just dumb," she says, fighting tears. "I feel like a terrible person. Now he'll never know how much I loved him. I'm mad at him for dying and leaving me and mad at God for taking him. Why did my dad have to die when I loved and needed him so much?"

Anger, too, is part of the process—and it may help to know this if you're feeling crazy because you're mad at someone you loved who died. You're mad at the loss of that person—and that's understandable. It isn't fair. It's a horrible loss for you. No wonder you're mad. Anyone would be.

GUILT

Guilt is a very common emotion for people to experience in the grief process. You may think about all the things you could have or should have said or done for the loved one you've lost. Or you may regret the arguments, the misunderstandings or the way you just assumed you'd have many years to share together. You may feel guilty for surviving the person—especially if that person is a sibling or friend whom you admired. You may feel that person deserved to live more than you do, had more to give the world than you do, and wonder why that person died and not you. Not coincidentally, you may feel some guilt over fleeting feelings of relief that it *was* your sibling or friend who died and not you. That happens a lot and doesn't mean you're a bad person. It just means you're human, like the rest of us!

You may also feel guilt about having moments of joy or feeling normal in the middle of the grief process. You may believe you're a terrible person because you're laughing at a joke or enjoying an outing with a friend when someone special to you is dead. Again, allowing ourselves to laugh and experience joy—joy in the moment or joy in memories—between the waves of pain will strengthen and sustain us in the grief process. Laughter, as well as tears, can be healing.

BEREAVEMENT

Bereavement is a time of tears, of longing, of realizing that, no matter how you may wish it were not so, your loved one is gone. You realize that there is nothing you can do but go on—and yet life without him or her seems impossibly sad and lonely. You find yourself crying for the lost love, the lost time together, for that irreplaceable person. And you cry for yourself—for the part of yourself that seemed to die a little, too, for the part of your life that will be forever altered by this loss. This is a deeply painful time, but a healing one.

ACCEPTANCE OF THE DEATH

This doesn't mean that you think it's just fine that this person died. It doesn't mean saying "Oh, OK, I'm over that. I'll get on with my life as if nothing ever happened." Acceptance doesn't mean forgetting.

What acceptance means is that you have raged, cried, talked, prayed—in essence, have worked hard—through your grief process and have come to some sort of understanding of your loss. You still won't like it. You may still have moments of tears—triggered by a remembered song, a birthday or holiday or a milestone in your life like graduation or your wedding—when you long for the presence of that special person. But you accept the fact of the death and the fact that, in some ways, your life has changed forever. You adapt to this change and go on—maybe always a little sadder, maybe always feeling that person missing from your life.

WHAT TO DO WHEN YOU'RE GRIEVING FOR SOMEONE YOU LOVE

✓ *Let your feelings happen.* Whatever your stage of the grief process, let it happen. You may feel like crying a lot—or not at all just now. There is no *right* way to grieve, only your way. Some people need more time than others to get past the initial shock. Some people need to be alone. Some need to be with others as they work through their grief. Let yourself feel anger if it comes up, realizing that this is a normal reaction to loss. Cry when you feel like it. Tears are normal and healing. They are *not* a sign of weakness and are as appropriate for men as for women. Trying to hold back tears because you think courage means stoicism may only prolong your pain. Your feelings are going to express themselves directly or indirectly (through physical symptoms or a clinical depression later on). It's best to let your feelings happen at a time when others are most likely to be supportive. If you bottle up your feelings and your grief erupts finally months or even years later, the understanding and support may not be there as much for you. Keep in mind that courage means walking through your pain, facing it, fully experiencing it and working it through.

✓ *Talk and share your feelings with others.* This may take both courage and effort. Some usual confidantes (e.g., a parent or parents) may not be as available to you if they are also grieving, and so you may need to reach out to others—preferably others who know how to listen instead of worrying about what to say to you. When someone you love has died, there's nothing that *can* be said to alleviate the pain. "I'm sorry" or "I love you" may soothe the pain, but listening when you need to express your grief may help most of all. You may need to be a little assertive about asking for a listening ear since many people may be afraid of upsetting you by bringing your loss up, or they may not be quite sure how to help.

Joyce, whose mother died of cancer when she was sixteen, remembers how it was for her just after her mother's death. "I was in a state of shock and wanted to talk to someone about the whole thing," she says. "I got on the phone and called several friends, who were very sympathetic, but scared. They assumed I just didn't feel like talking. They said something like 'Oh, Joyce, that's terrible. Let me know if there is anything I can do to help. I know you don't feel like talking now.' Only I *did*! Finally, I told that to one girlfriend. We were on the phone for over an hour and I told her all the details about what had just happened with my mother. I needed to talk about it because it was both terrible and awesome. We both cried during the conversation and it really helped to share that. But I had to ask because I knew my friend would not ask me 'How exactly did you mother die? What was it like? What happened when she actually died?' But those were the things I needed to talk about just then. Later, I needed to talk about feelings more like how I missed her and how scared I was without her, and I found several people who would listen—and that meant a lot. I didn't feel so alone."

It might also help to join a grief group for teenagers. These are available at counseling centers, churches and even at some high schools. Check with your school counselor, your clergyperson or the local family service counseling agencies to see what might be available in your area. When you're in a group with other teens who have experienced the death of someone important in their lives, you may feel very safe, accepted and understood. And that can help a lot.

✓ *Give yourself time*. It takes time to heal. There is no set "normal" time to grieve over the death of someone you love. So much depends on the relationship you had with the person who died, how that person died, how much support you have in your grieving process and how the death changed your life circumstances quite beyond the fact that you lost someone special to you. Healing is a gradual process, with pain softening over time. Although you will probably feel the loss of this person in many ways, at many times in your life, it won't always hurt as much as it does right now.

✓ *Realize that the grief process isn't a straight line, but a lot of steps forward and back.* You may have a few minutes or hours someday when you feel pretty OK, even happy. Then grief comes back in a wave of pain and longing. As time goes on, you find that the pain you feel can be intense, but it isn't constant. There may be times when you feel pretty good, but you may feel guilty about feeling good after suffering such a loss, or afraid to tell people that you're feeling fine today because they will expect you to be fine from now on—when you know your journey through grief is far from over. You may feel that it's crazy to be laughing about something when, overall, you're feeling so bad.

What you're feeling is normal and OK. Those moments of laughter and joy will give you strength for the painful times. The ability to laugh and to enjoy life between your moments of pain will help you to grow stronger and wiser as you work through this loss.

✓ *Take good care of yourself physically.* The stress of loss can have a major impact on your physical health, making you more susceptible to everything from headaches and stomachaches to frequent colds and even major illnesses. It is also not unusual to lose or gain a significant amount of weight—depending on whether you tend to lose your appetite or overeat in times of stress—and that can be a further health hazard. To prevent health problems making you feel even worse than you do already, take time to take care of yourself, even though you may be thinking "Why bother?" Try to eat nutritionally balanced meals even if you have little appetite. Get some kind of physical exercise every day. Walks can be wonderful because they give you time to think and, at the same time, to appreciate the beauty and/or familiarity of the world around you. And if you choose to walk with someone, this can be an excellent time to talk and share your feelings—taking care of yourself in several ways at once. Take warm, soothing baths or showers. Keep up your beauty and grooming routines. If you start looking bad, you'll feel even worse. Taking time to give yourself a manicure when your world is falling apart may seem incredibly stupid and pointless. But it may help give you a feeling of control when so much else is out of your control. You can't change the fact of your loved one's death. But you *do* have control over your hair and nails, and you can take control over what you eat and how and when you exercise. These small steps toward order in your life can be amazingly reassuring when everything else has changed so much.

✓ *Explore your spiritual beliefs and your curiosity about death.* When someone very close to you dies, you may wonder about a lot of things you're afraid to share with anyone because you're sure they will think you're being morbid or crazy or worse. But when you've shared so much with a person and suddenly they're gone, it's natural to wonder what may be happening with them physically or on a spiritual level. If you have questions about what happens to the body after death or what is involved in processes like embalming or cremation, ask the funeral director who was or is involved in taking care of those things for your family or friends. Most funeral directors are used to such questions—and in some areas where death education is offered in high schools, local morticians have answered many of these questions right in classes. So you're probably not the first person to ask. If you're too embarrassed, there are also some books about the physical process of death in your local library. If you find yourself obsessing about this for months, stuck with these thoughts about what happens to one's body, it may be time to talk with a counselor or therapist about your thoughts and concerns. But curiosity as you go through the grief process is very common.

It's even more common to wonder what death means and where your loved one is right now. If you're religious, you may find a great deal of comfort in your beliefs about heaven, an afterlife or reincarnation. If you're a skeptic about religion, you may find yourself curious and hopeful nonetheless and wanting to read about near-death experiences to get an idea of what the person you loved and lost has experienced or may be experiencing. You may be drawn to books about angels and the afterlife—books you might not have thought to pick up before. These books are in abundance in bookstores and on best-seller lists right now for a very good reason: the very large baby boomer population (quite possibly your parents if they were born between 1946 and 1964) is aging and their parents are dying. It's intensely painful to lose a parent at *any* age, and this large group of readers is eagerly buying anything that will help them to make sense of death and mortality—their loved ones' and their own. Although you may feel special pain, going through the experience of loss so early in life, you may also find comfort in many excellent books looking at the possibility of life hereafter.

It may also help to talk with someone who is deeply religious but who will respect your right to have your own beliefs. A compassionate minister, priest or rabbi or a pastoral counselor can help a lot. So can a youth counselor at your local church or synagogue.

If you start thinking that life isn't worth living and that your pain will only be resolved by joining your loved one in death, **get help immediately! Suicide is *not* the answer!** No matter how close you were, no matter how deep the loss you're feeling, killing yourself is not a tribute, not a sign of love. It will only intensify the pain of the other survivors. And deep down, if you are really honest about this, you *know* that the person you have lost would not want you to die, but to live your full life and to do and accomplish all you want and need to do in this lifetime. In many ways, the greatest tribute you can give to someone you love who has died is to live fully, honorably and lovingly—making the most of each day you have.

✓ *Accept the death in your own way.* Accepting the death of this person you love does not mean forgetting. To the contrary. When you accept the fact of death, you will be able to view that person's life as a whole—remembering the good times with loving appreciation even while you continue to mourn his or her passing in many ways. As you accept the fact that he or she is gone, you may feel free to remember the funny, touching, silly and courageous things about this person—memories that can make you smile through your tears, and, someday, simply smile.

Be open to letting your memories, your good feelings and your dreams help in your healing. Many people overlook the possibility that dreams can give you both comfort and insights as you grieve.

For example, when Kelsey's mother died suddenly of a heart attack, Kelsey was in school and never had a chance to say good-bye. She cried for months about the unfairness of her mother's early death. She fell into a profound depression, isolating herself from family and from friends. She found herself sobbing in the shower (where no one would hear and think she was crazy for not getting over her mother's death at a time when everyone else in her family seemed pretty much back to normal). Over and over, she raged at fate and at God: "Why? Why did this have to happen?"

One night Kelsey dreamed that she was swimming just off her family's favorite beach on the New Jersey shore. Suddenly her mother swam up beside her. Kelsey nearly leapt out of the water with joy. "Oh, Mama!" she cried. "Where have you been?"

Her mother looked nonchalant as she swam beside her. "Oh, just around," she said. "Never far away from you, darling." Then she disappeared under the water.

Kelsey dove down to retrieve her mother, dragged her up on the beach and prepared to give her CPR. Lying on the wet sand, her mother opened her eyes and looked at Kelsey with incredible love and tenderness. "If you love me . . . really love me . . . you'll let me go," she said quietly. "Do you love me enough to let me go?"

Tears slid down Kelsey's cheeks as she closed her eyes and whispered "Yes, Mama. Yes, I do."

When she opened her eyes, her mother was gone, leaving not even a faint impression in the wet sand. But Kelsey no longer felt alone. She felt a warm, all-encompassing peace that had eluded her before. She felt her mother's love and nearness and realized that this feeling was hers for a lifetime.

It was just a dream. But when Kelsey woke up—with tears still wet on her cheeks—she continued to feel the same sense of comfort and peace. It was with this dream, she insists, that her acceptance of her mother's death happened and her real healing began.

Accepting the death of someone you love may give you new appreciation for the precious moments of your own life. When you realize, with new finality, that life as you know it cannot go on forever, you may learn to savor life's pleasures, challenges and possibilities all the more.

"I never thought anything good would come out of my brother dying of leukemia at the age of nineteen," says seventeen-year-old Dov. "The moment he died was the saddest, most terrible moment of my life. I was certain I'd never be happy again. Impossible. But as I thought about how well and happily he lived his nineteen years, it inspired me to try to do the same. I live fully in each moment. I truly appreciate good times with friends, close times with family, just ordinary days. Eric is with me in my joy and in my passion for theater and in my appreciation of life. Besides being the best brother

I could have had, he gave me a great gift with his death: the realization that none of us knows how long we have to live and that every day is important. Every day counts. There are times when I still long for and cry for my brother. But I am also thankful for learning this lesson at a young age—and thankful for every day I am alive."

13

I Feel Awful and
I Still Don't Know Why

As he talks about pain and hopelessness, Jason looks at his hands and blushes. It is obvious that he is not only struggling with the weight of a major depression, but also deeply ashamed.

"The thing is . . . what makes me feel so stupid about this is that I have a good family, good friends, a good life," he says quietly. "I have no reason to feel as bad as I do. I've thought and tried to find a reason, but I can't. I feel awful and I still don't know why."

There are times when depression and other troubling feelings can't be explained by a major change or identifiable problem in your life.

There are even times when your life is pretty good but *you* feel really bad. This can be an especially painful experience, because there may be no guidelines for getting better, no path to take for healing the way you could if your depression stemmed from a lost love, a parental divorce or the death of someone close to you.

If life is reasonably good, but you're feeling incredibly bad, you're also less likely to get the support you would get from others if your life were quite visibly in shambles.

This is a time when you may really believe you're crazy for feeling so bad, since it's unclear even to you *why* you feel this way. Life may seem so out of control that you begin to feel hopeless and helpless, and even suicidal.

How can you feel so bad for no apparent reason?

The answer may be that you're suffering from a chemical imbalance in your brain. This may sound frightening and unusual, but it is quite common. How does this happen?

Vital information that regulates feelings, thoughts and behavior is transmitted to the brain cells by the nervous system through the release of chemical substances called neurotransmitters. These chemicals are released at nerve terminals in your body and cause an electrical chain reaction of sorts from one nerve ending to another. There is a part of the brain that is associated with emotions. Here, the brain-function neurotransmitters are amino acid compounds called biogenic amines. These substances include serotonin and norepinephrine.

What does all this have to do with you and your troubling feelings?

Some scientists believe that an imbalance of these chemicals in the brain might be linked to depression in some people. Studies have found that an imbalance of serotonin may lead to depressive symptoms such as irritability, anxiety and sleep problems. Fatigue and a depressed mood can result from an imbalance of norepinephrine.

Who gets such chemical imbalances and why?

Some researchers believe that a tendency to have an imbalance of the brain's neurotransmitters may be an inherited characteristic. There have been a number of interesting studies exploring the possible genetic basis of depression in some people.

For example, in 1993 Dr. Anu Sharma of the Search Institute in Minnesota reported early findings of a 775-family study that examined patterns of depression in adopted teenagers, their birth mothers and their adoptive mothers. The results? The teens' depression scores were strongly similar to those of their birth mothers while researchers found zero correlation between the teens' depression and that of the adoptive mother.

Other studies of adopted children have found that even if raised in adoptive homes where the parents are not depressed, the adoptees have three times greater risk of depression if their biological relatives suffered from depression.

Studies of twins raised apart have also provided interesting comparisons of genetic versus environmental influences. It has been found that if one identical twin suffers from a depressive disorder, the other twin has a 60 to 70 percent chance of sharing that disorder—even if the two were raised by separate families.

What can help this biologically based depression?

There are several kinds of help that are useful, including treatment with antidepressant medications. A number of antidepressants work by altering the action of amines in the brain, thus correcting existing chemical imbalances.

Many people who are depressed have serious doubts about taking these drugs and struggle to feel better with everyday coping strategies. However, if you're suffering from a clinical depression (see Chapter Two for a complete description of clinical depression), particularly if it seems to be due to an imbalance of neurotransmitters, you may need more help than your own best efforts to cope with your feelings.

WHAT TO DO IF YOU'RE FEELING BAD AND YOU DON'T KNOW WHY

✓ *See your physician for a physical examination.* This is important for several reasons. First, there are a number of physical conditions that can have a link with depression. These include mononucleosis, hypothyroidism, problems with adrenal glands, and diabetes. It's also important to know that some medications you may be taking (like birth control pills or diet pills) can have side effects that include depression. A physical examination and consultation with your physician will explore these possible causes of your feeling so bad without knowing why. Another reason to check with your physician first: when you're feeling so bad, the prospect of trying to find a good mental health professional may be overwhelming. If you feel comfortable with your family doctor, seeking help here can be a vital first step, and your physician may be able to help you the rest of the way— e.g., by referring you to a mental health professional experienced in treating depression, and possibly working with this person if you need to have antidepressant drugs prescribed.

✓ *Be open to the option of antidepressant drug therapy.* Many people resist the idea of antidepressant drugs for a number of reasons: fear of the side effects of the drugs themselves, shame at having to consult a psychiatrist to get a prescription and shame over needing a drug to regulate feelings and/or behavior. Much resistance comes from the fact that most people don't understand what antidepressant drugs do and why they're necessary at times.

There may be times when you feel so bad that the best psychotherapist can't help you the way you need to be helped—nor can your best friend or mother—and the medication can simply put you in a position to make better use of the help of others and your own efforts to help yourself. Ideally, a clinical depression is not treated by drugs alone, but by a combination of antidepression medication (perhaps for only a while) and psychotherapy.

It's also important to know that you don't necessarily have to visit a psychiatrist to obtain an antidepressant. However, if at all possible, we do recommend this, because psychiatrists treat depression and prescribe antidepressants much more frequently than do family physicians. That said, if you have a physician—an adolescent medicine specialist, family physician, internist or pediatrician—whom you trust and who has experience with treating depression and prescribing antidepressants (or who is willing to work in consultation with a psychiatrist who will monitor drug dosage to determine what would work best for you), your comfort level may be greater, at least initially, with this doctor, because you know him or her already.

There are a number of types of antidepressants. Most work by restoring proper balance to the neurotransmitters in the brain. The newer antidepressants—such as Prozac, Paxil and Zoloft—are reputed to have fewer side effects than older medications like tricyclic antidepressants.

There has been some question recently regarding how well tricyclic antidepressants work in adolescents. In a 1993 study of treatment for adolescent depression, Dr. Anne C. Petersen of the University of Minnesota found that in several controlled studies, tricyclic antidepressants did not appear to help depressed teenagers all that much. Several earlier studies also cast some doubt on the effectiveness of some antidepressants on adolescents.

The researchers are still looking for the reason why this may be so. Dr. Petersen and her colleagues are now exploring biological differences between teenagers and adults as well as the fact that depressed teenagers may have more serious forms of depressive disorders than adults.

At this writing, there do not appear to be any studies looking at the impact of the newer antidepressants on teenagers. These may or may not be more helpful to you. And you could well be one of the individual teens who find even an older-generation antidepressant helpful. This is something you need to discuss with your physician and is one of the reasons why we suggest consulting with a physician who is experienced in prescribing these medications to teenagers.

These pills aren't magic, in the sense that they will not make you feel better immediately (it usually takes from about ten days to several weeks before you feel any difference at all), and they won't instantly solve any problems you have. But they may enable you to regain enough hope and resourcefulness to help yourself in new ways.

✓ *Be open to the option of psychotherapy.* If you're seriously depressed, psychotherapy is an excellent option in addition to or instead of drug therapy (should you and your doctor decide drug therapy just isn't for you). Psychotherapy can be a comfort. It can also help you to discover issues, experiences and feelings that may be related to your current pain. Many people are scared and embarrassed to go get professional mental help, fearing that this will mean being labeled "crazy" for sure. But, as we will see in the next chapter, there are many different kinds of therapy and therapists available, and one or more of these may be just right (and feel just right) for you.

Remember: there is nothing wrong with needing and getting help. Such help may, in fact, save your life.

Part III

GETTING AND GIVING HELP

14

Getting Professional Help

Maybe it was a strong suggestion from a teacher or school counselor or from your physician or a parent.

Maybe it was a gentle hint from a friend: "Maybe you ought to talk to someone who could really help you in a way that I can't."

Maybe you have been thinking that you need to talk with someone about feelings that are interfering with your life, such as:

- Depressed or irritable mood most of the day, nearly every day
- Loss of interest or pleasure in activities you have always enjoyed before
- Inability to concentrate
- A change in eating habits that has led to a significant weight loss or gain (a change of more than 5 percent of body weight in one month), a diminished or increased appetite

- Withdrawal from friends or alienation of them with your outbursts of anger or irritability
- Having trouble sleeping at night or feeling like sleeping all the time
- Feelings of restlessness or being slowed down
- Feelings of persistent fatigue
- Feelings of worthlessness or excessive or inappropriate guilt on a daily basis
- Recurrent thoughts of death (not just fear of dying), thoughts of suicide, with or without a specific plan and/or suicide attempts
- Feeling you really need to talk with someone right now about an issue or problem you're afraid to bring up with family or friends

All of these feelings—some of them signs of major depression—are very good reasons to see a mental health professional.

Yet many people, even those who *know* their feelings are more than they can handle alone, balk at actually going to a therapist. Many—maybe even you, too—have questions and concerns like the following:

❑ *What would my friends think if they knew I was seeing a shrink?* Some of your friends may be in therapy, too, and just haven't told you. While seeking psychotherapy does not have the stigma it used to have, many young people worry that their friends will tease them or think they're crazy for seeing a mental health professional. You don't necessarily have to tell your friends if you know they would not understand.

Another thing to think about: while your friends' opinions are important to you, getting the help you need has to be most important to you right now. Keep in mind, too, that helping yourself in therapy may improve your friendships as your symptoms of depression and distress diminish.

❏ *What if the therapist tells my parents everything?* Psychotherapists of all kinds follow certain ethical and professional codes and one of the most important of these is confidentiality. This applies, in most states, even if you're a minor. If you have any doubts about what the regulations are where you live, ask the therapist before you tell him or her anything.

There are a few instances when a therapist is bound by law to break confidentiality: first, if you are in immediate danger of harming yourself—e.g., if you are suicidal and have a plan, the therapist may notify your family so that they can also help to protect your life at this time. The therapist is also obligated, by law, to report to the proper authorities anything you may tell him or her about physical or sexual abuse. Third, in some states, the therapist also has a duty to warn a potential victim or victims if you appear to pose a serious threat to the life of another.

In most instances, however, what you say to the therapist will (and *must*) stay between the two of you.

❏ *What if I'm not comfortable talking with a stranger about my private thoughts and feelings?*

That's understandable. But it may help to know that psychotherapists, like physicians, have heard just about everything and it's difficult if not impossible to shock or surprise them. The therapist is not there to judge you, but to listen and to help you find new insights and ways to help yourself.

After you get past your initial uneasiness, you may find it easier to talk with the therapist about private things than it is to talk with some of your friends. After all, in a way, you care more about what your friends think than what the therapist thinks of you, and also there isn't the danger that your therapist will go blab a secret all over school.

❏ *I've heard from a friend that therapy can make you feel worse. Who needs* that?? While it's true that you may explore some very painful feelings in therapy, it's important to realize that you'll be doing this in the presence of someone who knows how to help you through these feelings and who will provide a safe place for you to experience such pain.

These, by the way, are not feelings that therapy causes. These are the feelings that are causing you to feel so bad and maybe so out of control now. The difference between just living with the feelings and dealing with them in therapy is that, instead of trying to ignore them or distract yourself from them, in therapy you will be facing them. By facing and working through this pain in therapy, you will begin to heal and to feel better.

❑ *How can an adult really understand how I feel?*
A psychotherapist has special training in understanding people's feelings. Some therapists are
especially interested in working with teenagers
and particularly sensitive to the problems and issues you're facing. Those of us who *choose* to
work with adolescents (as psychotherapists or as
physicians) usually do so because we genuinely
like teenagers and want to understand you and
help you. We may be all different ages—some of
us are close to you in age and some of us are
closer to your parents' ages—but we all share a
desire to help you to help yourself.

❑ *Therapy takes too much time. I don't have time to
go to therapy all the time—for years! What do I
do about that?* Actually, you're coming to therapy at a good time, because brief therapy—typically six to twenty sessions—is increasingly
popular among both those seeking therapy and
their insurance companies.

If you are severely depressed, suicidal or have
a complicated family situation, you may need to
have more than brief therapy. But most people
these days will see a therapist once a week for a
few weeks or months and find the help they
need.

The main point of therapy, after all, is to help
you to develop the insights and skills to help
yourself. The object is *not* (or should not) be to
make you dependent on therapy for years to
come.

❑ *I hear therapy is expensive. How can I afford it?*
Some therapists *are* expensive, but you can get

excellent help without blowing your family's (or your own) budget.

Many insurance plans have mental health benefits and are particularly inclined to cover most of the cost of brief therapy. You family's insurance may offer such benefits.

There is also low-cost therapy available—therapists who charge a "sliding scale" for therapy based on ability to pay. You may find one of these by calling a local hot line or your local family service agency.

❏ *My parents don't believe in therapy.* Many parents are also victims of the old mind-set that seeking mental health help is a terrible and shameful thing. They may also be feeling protective—not wanting you to be hurt or harmed in any way— or guilty that they can't seem to help you—as much as they would like to—or afraid the therapist will consider them bad parents because you need therapy. Some parents, too, hesitate to allow therapy because they're afraid it will change you in ways they can't tolerate.

If you need and want help from a mental health professional and your parents are reluctant to agree to this, it might be useful if a concerned teacher, school counselor, clergyperson or your family physician could talk to them and help them to see how this might benefit not only you, but also the family. It might be of assistance, too, if they could meet the therapist with whom you hope to work. They may be reassured that this therapist will be truly helpful to you.

WHO ARE THERAPISTS AND HOW DO I FIND ONE?

There are several different kinds of mental health professionals.

The type you choose may depend on your particular problem or the kind of therapy you would like to have and may also depend on the type of therapist your insurance company prefers (some carriers insist that you see a psychiatrist or a psychologist, while other insurance providers prefer master's-degree-level therapists like marriage and family counselors or licensed clinical social workers).

Who are these therapists and what are the differences between them?

Psychiatrists have M.D. degrees. That is, they are medical doctors with specialized post–medical school training in treating mental and emotional illness. They can treat people with mild to severe disorders who may require medication. At the present time, only psychiatrists, as medical doctors, can directly prescribe drugs such as antidepressants. But that doesn't mean that your therapist has to be a psychiatrist if you might need medication. Many nonmedical mental health professionals— such as psychologists, marriage/family counselors and licensed clinical social workers—have cooperative arrangements with psychiatrists to consult with and prescribe medication as needed for their clients.

Look for a psychiatrist who is certified by the American Board of Psychiatry and Neurology, which means that he or she is a fully licensed doctor with special training in psychiatry and passing marks in a series of special examinations to determine competence in the field.

(However, since this credential is fairly new, some excellent older psychiatrists may not be board-certified.)

A *psychologist* has a doctoral-level degree—generally a Ph.D. or a Psy.D. in clinical or counseling psychology. In order to be licensed as a psychologist, this professional must have completed four to six years of graduate study plus several more years of supervised clinical training (a total of three thousand hours) and received passing marks on a special licensing examination in order to practice.

A psychologist can be a good choice of treatment for emotional problems and disorders. Psychologists tend to be experienced in testing and assessment, which can be useful when extensive testing is required, needed or suggested as part of your treatment.

A *licensed marriage/family/child counselor* (sometimes called an MFCC or MFT, for marriage and family therapist) has at least a master's degree in clinical or counseling psychology. You would see the designation M.A., MFCC or M.A., MFT after one of these counselors' names. What this means is that the therapist has had two to three years of graduate-level training and a certain amount of supervised clinical experience. In California, for example, an MFCC/MFT-level therapist must complete seventy-two quarter units or 48 semester units of graduate study (twice the typical units for a purely academic master's degree in psychology) plus three thousand hours of supervised clinical experience (which translates to several years, typically) before being eligible to take a difficult licensing exam and start his or her own practice.

This type of therapist may well do individual or couple

or family therapy, but is particularly well trained in doing family systems therapy, which means understanding and treating the family as a system, seeing that your problems and feelings may stem from what is happening within your family and also looking at patterns of feeling and behaving that may have been present through several generations of your family relationships. All of this can help you to understand yourself and your own feelings better and also, if you are getting family therapy rather than individual therapy, to help your family relate better to one another and communicate in ways that are more helpful to everyone.

A *psychiatric social worker (MSW or LCSW)* has at least a master's degree in social work, along with supervised clinical experience. He or she is especially trained to evaluate and work with emotional problems in a social context. Some psychiatric social workers have additional certification from the Academy of Certified Social Workers. This certification means that the therapist's degree is from an accredited social work program and that the social worker has completed the required supervised experience and passed a national qualifying examination. Social workers, like the other mental health professionals already mentioned, must be licensed by the state.

That is important: look for a therapist who has a degree from a fully accredited school and who is properly licensed.

If you decide to go to a clinic or agency for low-cost therapy, your therapist might be a graduate student in training to be a psychologist, MFCC or social worker. This person is doing a traineeship or practicum prior to getting a master's degree. Or he or she may be doing an internship *after* receiving an M.A. or M.S.W., while working toward licensing and/or a doctoral degree. Many of these newer therapists do very fine work and are strictly supervised by licensed therapists. The cost of this therapy may be considerably less than therapy with an established professional (while getting valuable input from the supervisor who *is* an established professional).

How do you find a therapist?

If you are feeling suicidal and need help quickly, call your local suicide prevention center or local hot line for instant help and later referral to longer-term therapy.

Beyond emergency situations, there are many ways to find a competent therapist including:

- Your family physician
- Local mental health associations
- Local branches of national associations for mental health professionals, such as the American Psychiatric Association, the American Psychological Association, the American Association for Marriage and Family Therapists or the Academy of Certified Social Workers
- The graduate psychology department of a local university, or the professional services department or alumni affairs department of the nearest graduate professional school of psychology
- A friend or relative who has had therapy and whose therapist may be able to refer you to a colleague
- Your local family service agency, your family's HMO or EAP program

Once you have the name of one or more possible therapists, call them to make an initial appointment to see if you might work well together. Don't get discouraged if you find that the first therapist you talk with just isn't for you. Keep in mind that mental health professionals, despite having solid professional training in common, are as varied in personal style, outlook and personality as the general population. The first therapist you meet may feel just right for you. But, if not, don't stop looking. Also, your own uneasiness with the *idea* of therapy may make *any* therapist feel wrong at first.

While it's common to feel a little uneasy when you first meet with a therapist, you will know, deep down, after spending an hour or so with this person whether or not you will be able to work together. Does this person listen well? Is this person likely to encourage you to work at seeking your own solutions (instead of claiming to have all the answers)? Do you feel that, once you get over your initial uneasiness, you could work with this person? Then you may have a good match!

HOW TO GET THE MOST OUT OF THERAPY

✓ *Give therapy (and your therapist) a fair chance.* Therapy isn't a quick fix, an instant answer to all your problems. It's hard work—on the part of the therapist, certainly, but mostly by you, or in the case of family therapy, by the therapist and the whole family.

Keep in mind that it takes time and effort to make changes in the ways you feel, think and relate to others, even if you're getting brief therapy.

If you bail out after one or two or three sessions and announce that therapy isn't for you, you're not giving it or *yourself* a fair chance.

✓ *Don't sabotage the therapy.* The best therapist in the world can't help you if you won't let him or her.

How do some teens sabotage therapy?

- By lying to the therapist or refusing to disclose information that could help the therapist help them
- By sulking through sessions and refusing to say *anything* (this can be tempting if your parents made you go to a therapist and you don't want to be there)
- By missing appointments or constantly coming late
- By trying to uphold a certain image with the therapist and not getting into information they feel might make them look bad in his or her eyes
- By trying to entice the therapist into telling them that they are right even when they know they're not (You have friends who will tell you this for free. You're paying a therapist to help you work through your problems and troubling feelings, not to admire you constantly.)
- By flirting with the therapist and/or trying to make the relationship a personal one rather than a professional one. (While it's not unusual to have warm feelings or even sexual fantasies about a therapist who works well with you, it's important to know that therapists cannot ethically have per-

sonal or sexual relationships with their clients.) Continuing to push for a personal relationship may keep you and your therapist from working well together or, in fact, working together at all.

✓ *Be open to change.* The object of therapy is not to change your whole personality and everything about you. However, your therapist may encourage you to make changes in how you think or feel about yourself— e.g., working to stop negative patterns of thinking in favor of a more positive approach, finding things to appreciate about yourself instead of always tearing yourself down, finding ways to communicate differing feelings to your parents without yelling or insulting them, or taking the risk of being different from your friends when you need to be.

Change can be scary and far from easy. Being open to change enables you to make changes in your life that are beneficial to you. If you really think about it, there are certain changes and risks well worth trying for your own growth, your own sanity, your own peace of mind and your own journey away from despair toward hope.

And helping you to build the strength, insight, courage and resourcefulness to find this new hope is what good therapy is all about.

15

I Have a Friend Who . . .

I have a friend who is so upset about breaking up with her boyfriend that her grades and her life are just the pits. I keep telling her she should be happy to be rid of him, but she just cries and defends him. I really care about her, but it's getting hard to help her. What can I do?

—Jill B.

I have a friend who was talking about killing himself. It scared me because someone at our school killed himself last year. All of his friends knew he was planning to do it, but nobody knew what to do or told anyone who might have helped. What I did with my friend was I told a teacher and also my friend's mom. Well, now he's really mad at me for telling and doesn't want to be friends anymore. I feel really bad. I thought I was doing the right thing, but now I'm not so sure.

—Brent K.

What Jill and Brent describe are common challenges when you have a friend in pain or in trouble: it's hard to know what to say and do and whether to tell someone else if your friend seems to be in serious trouble.

HOW TO HELP A FRIEND IN TROUBLE

✓ *Listening may be the greatest gift you can give a friend.* Think about what helps most when you're upset. Most of us really want someone to listen and understand how we're feeling. Lots of advice or stories about how you handled something you feel is similar are much less helpful than just listening and giving your full attention to a friend who is troubled. When you listen carefully, you can get clues to knowing how best to help your friend and questions to ask to begin to help your friend find his or her own solution. Most of all, though, listening will help your friend to feel that someone cares. And there are times when that means everything.

✓ *Choose your words carefully.* If, like Jill, you have a friend who is suffering through a romantic breakup, don't volunteer your low opinion of his or her former love and thus put your friend in the position of defending the old flame. Instead, encourage your friend to reflect on and get on with the grieving and recovery process, by asking questions like these:

"What do you miss about him/her? And what *don't* you miss?"

"What could you have done differently?"

"What did you learn from this?"

"What do you wish would happen? And what do you think is likely to happen? How bad would that be? How would you cope with that?"

These and a myriad of other questions that might be appropriate to your friend's situation will keep the focus on him or her and keep your friend thinking in an active way.

This doesn't mean that you bombard your friend with questions. But a gentle question, that keeps him or her thinking instead of sitting mired in despair, can help.

✓ *Be affirmative, not critical.* It is possible to point out a pattern of negative thinking or other behavior not beneficial to your friend without criticizing. This is particularly important at a time when your friend may be feeling so vulnerable.

You can still get your message across to a friend who is wishing her abusive ex-boyfriend would take her back or to a friend who insists on putting himself down at every opportunity (with predictably depressing results).

What you need to do is to substitute affirmative statements for ones that sound more critical. For example:

Instead of: "You have the worst taste in men! He's awful. Lose him! What's the matter with you? Are you crazy?"

You might say: "I really wish you could meet someone who will treat you the way you deserve to be treated—with love and respect. I get really angry when I see someone treating you the way Doug has. As your friend, I want so much more for you."

Instead of: "Yeah, well, so maybe you have this fault or that fault, but don't bore me with it. I know what your faults are . . . You know what really bothers me is when you talk too much . . ."

You might say: "I get upset when you put yourself down. I wish that you could see yourself as I see you. I think you're terrific and I particularly enjoy being with you when . . ."

Affirmative words from a trusted friend can go a long way to make inroads into the inertia that depression can cause. Even if your friend is self-critical over a very real mistake, there are affirmative ways to agree with him or her that will make your friend feel less hopeless and alone. For example:

Instead of: "Yeah, you sure screwed up this time."

You might say: "That's an easy kind of mistake to make. We've all done that or come close to doing that. What do you think your best option is right now?"

Helping your friend to feel less alone and giving him or her thoughts or ideas about a solution or resolution in the form of a question might help, once again, to keep your friend from getting mired in hopelessness and a sense of powerlessness.

✓ *Don't rush to give advice.* What works for you may not work for your friend. Also, even if what you think is best definitely looks like the best possible plan of action right now, you should present it as an option, not a mandate: Instead of "You should . . . ," suggest "Have you thought about . . ." That way, the person is more likely to hear what you're saying instead of angrily rejecting any advice (which can happen when one is feeling really angry and helpless and down).

Quite often, a person really doesn't want advice. He

or she knows what needs to be done. It's quite likely that your friend only wants someone who matters to him or her to listen and to care.

✓ *If your friend needs more help than you can give, encourage him or her to get adult and/or professional help.* This would apply if your friend is showing signs of a major clinical depression (see Chapter Two), is feeling overwhelmed with problems and seeking solutions in ways that are harmful or if your friend is feeling suicidal.

If your friend is depressed, but not suicidal, gently suggest talking with an adult who can help, or a professional counselor. If he or she resists the idea of going to a mental health professional, suggest that your friend check with his or her physician to see if mono or some other undiagnosed medical condition might be causing him or her to feel so bad. This may feel less threatening to your friend and may get him or her into the health care system, where some help can be obtained and possibly a referral from the physician to a mental health professional.

If your friend is feeling suicidal, and especially if he or she appears to have a plan or is beginning to give away personal belongings, strongly urge your friend to get help. Offer to go with him or her, or find a phone number for the local suicide prevention center or crisis hot line—even dial the number for your friend.

This is also a time for you to risk telling someone who can help if your friend will not or cannot reach out for adult help. Even if you risk making your friend angry or risk his or her rejection, this is a risk worth taking if it means saving your friend's life.

BREAKING THE SILENCE AND GETTING HELP

Deciding to tell someone that your friend is in serious trouble—contemplating suicide or otherwise posing a danger to himself or herself or others—is a clear, but tough decision. Like Brent, you may be thinking that it makes sense to tell an adult so that your friend can get the help he or she so obviously needs. On the other hand, you're scared of making your friend angry at you, perhaps so angry that it will mean the end of your friendship. It is a risk. But there are times when your friend's safety must come first—especially when your friend's life or the lives and well-being of others may be at stake.

If possible, don't wait until the crisis has reached a dangerous peak, when your friend has a gun to his or her head. Hear danger in suicide threats (instead of just dismissing them) so that you—and your friend—will have more time to find just the right kind of help.

Whom do you tell? It depends somewhat on the crisis. In a suicidal crisis, time may be crucial and the suicide prevention center as well as parents need to know as soon as possible.

If your friend is feeling bad enough to alarm you but is not obviously suicidal or homicidal, there are a number of adults who might help: parents (yours or your friend's), an especially understanding teacher, a clergyperson or any other adult you trust and who is in a position to help your friend. As well as offering support, this person may be able to find a mental health professional to further assist your friend.

It's true that telling an adult what's happening with your friend may not inspire gratitude from your friend, immediately or ever. Like Brent's friend, yours may be angry and rejecting—at least temporarily.

But Brent—and you—did the right thing by telling, even if your friend claims it was a false alarm or a complete overreaction on your part. Even if that turns out to be true, you have done the right thing. It is far better, after all, to risk your friend's wrath and your own embarrassment than to pass up the opportunity to help save a life.

16

You're Not Crazy . . . You're Normal!

If you're feeling . . .

- Helpless and alone after a romantic breakup
- Frustrated and depressed over what feels like a significant failure
- Like your world is coming apart because your family is changing
- Sad and isolated because you're different from your peers
- Stressed out with no relief in sight
- Devastated by the death of someone you love
- Depressed for reasons you can't pinpoint, yet your pain is very real . . .

. . . or similar feelings, you're simply human. We all have times of feeling sadness, uncertainty and loneliness. We have all been disappointed (even devastated for a time) by a romantic breakup. We have all felt stress, a sense of failure, the pain of being different in some way. And many of us have experienced the heartbreak of a loved one dying.

On the other hand, most of us have known the joy of falling in love, the excitement and warmth of connecting with others in friendship, the thrill of discovering all we share with one another, the satisfaction of learning or succeeding at something (maybe after a real struggle) and the warm and loving memories that come from taking the risk of being close to others, even though that closeness can bring sorrow as well as joy.

Just being alive and being human exposes us to all these joys, sorrows, challenges and possibilities.

The fact is, contrary to the fairy tales, no one lives "happily ever after." Life is filled with happiness and pain in varying measures. Taking time to appreciate the good times and nurture ourselves during the trying times can make the difference between feeling that life is unfair, out of control, not worth the effort or hopeless, and feeling empowered and optimistic about the future.

Whether or not you have been able—in the course of time or while reading this book—to resolve your pain yourself or with the help of others . . . there is hope.

Whether or not you feel 100 percent better, whether or not the situations causing or contributing to your pain have changed significantly (or at all) . . . there is hope.

You can find hope in your own ability to help yourself through the toughest times. You can help yourself most in these ways:

✓ *Be gentle with yourself.* Treat yourself with the same tender loving care you would give your best friend. Care for yourself in a multitude of ways—from good nutrition and regular exercise to making time for fun and not giving yourself a hard time over mistakes. Don't beat yourself up when things go wrong or when you make a mistake. Give yourself permission to be human—like the rest of us. Don't assume or insist that a situation is hopeless because you can't see an instant solution or find something to make yourself feel better right away. Most pain takes time to heal . . . and being gentle with yourself can help that healing a lot.

✓ *Don't label yourself.* Name-calling hurts—and that includes self-labeling like "You're so stupid! How could you *do* that?" or "You're crazy! Why can't you just get over things and go on?"

Would you say these things to someone you love? It's time—especially if you're in pain—to love yourself the way you love close friends and family.

Give yourself the freedom to make mistakes and learn from them.

Give yourself the time you need to work through painful feelings.

Don't compare yourself with others whose lives and ways of being seem to be perfect. No one or no life is perfect. Some people *seem* to have it all together in a crisis. But if you were to look more closely, you might see that the person was still numb from shock or that he or she keeps feelings very private, or denies and doesn't deal with painful feelings. And if someone truly does seem to cope well in a crisis, maybe you can learn something valuable from watching how that person handles his or her crisis situation. Perhaps that person is likely to say, "This is a terrible situation and I feel really bad. Let's see what I can do to make things at least a little better for myself and those I love."

This is *not* a time to criticize yourself and pin hurtful labels on yourself. Not now. Not *ever*.

✓ *Embrace and work through your pain.* Some people will do anything to avoid pain, including using alcohol or drugs, food or sex or simply staying extremely busy and distracted. None of those instant "solutions" really helps to solve problems or alleviate pain long-term, and most make your pain and your situation far worse. By avoiding your pain, you also avoid solutions and possibilities for growth.

Pain doesn't necessarily make you a better person. Sometimes it just makes you sadder. Or tired. But learning to deal with a difficult situation and with pain when it comes can make you wiser, stronger and more compassionate.

In order to learn and grow, however, you need to embrace your pain and work through it.

That can mean really letting yourself feel the full brunt of pain—crying, grieving, expressing anger—maybe alone or maybe with someone you trust, when a romance ends or parents divorce or someone you love dies.

Embracing your pain can mean facing the fact that it's more than you can handle alone—and reaching out for help, from family and friends and perhaps even from a professional therapist.

It can mean giving yourself time to go through all the steps of loss and grief—from denial to anger to sadness to acceptance.

It can mean giving yourself the freedom to cope with a crisis by experiencing the full range of your feelings: crying when you must, laughing when you can between the moments of pain.

Finding the courage to embrace and work through your pain—no matter how horrifying it may look and feel—can keep you in charge of your own life and keep you from feeling overwhelmed by the crises that come to all of us.

Remember that as long as there is life, there is hope. Hope thrives when you feel in charge of your life. And you're never more in charge than when you're embracing all that life brings you—the pain and the joy—and growing from all these feelings and experiences!

INDEX

of gays/lesbians, 89
illness/disability of, 24
step/half-siblings, 61
Single parenthood, 80–81, 82,
83–84
Sleep problems, 14, 182
Social worker, psychiatric, 189–
190
Spermicidal jelly, 79
Spirituality, 122–123, 166–168
Sports, 144
Stepparents, 61, 62, 64, 65
Stepsiblings, 61
Stress, 102–125
college admissions process
and, 110–111
family, 24, 59, 115
friendships and, 105, 106,
107, 118–119
levels of, 103–104
parental expectations and,
106, 115–116
parental goals and, 117–118
perfectionism and, 106, 109,
116, 119–120
physical symptoms of, 107–
108
reduction, 108–125
schedule and, 121–122
school, 104, 105–106, 112–
115
sources of, 104–107, 108
Suicide
after death of loved one, 168
hot line, 9, 53, 190
psychotherapy and, 183

reporting threats of, 194,
198, 199–200
thoughts of, 9, 14, 41, 42,
53, 91, 182
Support groups
for gay/lesbian teens, 97–98
grief, 164
for teens with alcoholic
parents, 130–131
Support systems, friends as,
123–124, 163–164
Syphilis, 74

T
Teacher relations, 112–115
Torvill, Jane, 109
Tricyclic antidepressants, 177
Twin studies
of depression, 174
of gays/lesbians, 89

U
Uribe, Virginia, 97–98

V
Volunteer work, 148

W
Wallerstein, Judith, 4, 56
Weight gain/loss, 13, 14, 143,
165–166, 181
Worthlessness, feelings of, 14,
182

Z
Zoloft, 177

ABOUT THE AUTHORS

Kathy McCoy, Ph.D., is an award-winning author and behavioral expert. A former columnist for *Seventeen* magazine and a former editor of *'Teen*, she has written ten books and hundreds of articles for national magazines, newspapers and professional journals such as *Redbook, Reader's Digest, The New York Times, Family Circle, Ladies' Home Journal, Glamour, Mademoiselle, TV Guide* and *The Journal of Clinical Child Psychology*. Dr. McCoy is the coordinator of Clinical Proficiencies at California School of Professional Psychology, Los Angeles, and an admissions counselor for Northwestern University. She has made numerous appearances on national television shows including *Today, The Oprah Winfrey Show, Geraldo, Hour Magazine, Sally Jessy Raphael* and *Sonya Live*. She is also an on-line expert specializing in adolescent psychology for the National Parenting Center. She lives in Valencia, California.

Charles Wibbelsman, M.D., the award-winning author of three books and former "Dear Doctor" columnist for *'Teen* magazine, is a nationally prominent adolescent medicine specialist. He is chief of the Teen-Age Clinic at Kaiser Permanente Medical Center in San Francisco, a facility that treats approximately one-third of the total adolescent population of that city. He is an associate professor of pediatrics at the University of California, San Francisco Medical School, and president of the Northern California chapter of the Society for Adolescent Medicine. He also serves on the San Francisco Superintendent of Schools Advisory Committee.

Dr. Wibbelsman is a popular guest on national television shows, and has made numerous appearances on *Today, The Oprah Winfrey Show, Dr. Ruth, Hour Magazine* and *Sonya Live*. He is also an on-line expert specializing in adolescent health for the National Parenting Center. He lives in San Francisco.